The Minor Poems
of
John Milton

Illustrated by

A. Garth Jones

A facsimile reprint by

The Wildhern Press 2008

Published by

The Wildhern press

131 High St.
Teddington
Middlesex TW11 8HH

ISBN 978-184830902-9

THE MINOR POEMS
OF JOHN MILTON

L'ALLEGRO

The Minor Poems
of JOHN MILTON

ILLUSTRATED AND
DECORATED BY
A. GARTH JONES

LONDON
GEORGE BELL & SONS
1898.

Prefatory Note.

In illustrating the shorter poems of Milton the maker of these designs has naturally chosen those subjects that most appealed to him. In interpretation and execution he has striven to keep to what he conceives to be the Miltonic spirit, and has aimed generally at avoiding incident as likely to obscure that intention. For the same reason he has dispensed with abundance of merely decorative detail; the marked sanity and severity of Milton's writing seeming to be incompatible with the elaborate and often intricate design so much in vogue at the present day, whereby the poetic feeling in decoration is in danger of degenerating into a commonplace formalism.

In Milton's work there is a rare combination of graceful scholarship and classic method with the high and severe ethical ideals of the Puritan, which is perhaps hardly expressible in the medium of the draughtsman's art; and if he has leant rather to the severer side and the more solemn aspect of the poet's work, it is in the belief that this aspect is the one which presents itself to the great mass of his readers. The charm of Milton is chiefly of an intellectual kind,

PREFATORY NOTE

appealing to the thinker and the scholar, and in the eyes of such the designer would hope that his work, deficient though it may be in accessory graces, will not be found out of sympathy with the spirit of the poet.

October, 1898.

CONTENTS.

EARLY POEMS.

CONTENTS

SONNETS.

Illustrations.

ILLUSTRATIONS

ILLUSTRATIONS

ILLUSTRATIONS

ZEPHYR WITH AURORA PLAYING
AS HE MET HER ONCE A-MAYING

POEMS BY JOHN MILTON

ON THE DEATH OF A FAIR INFANT, DYING OF A COUGH

I

O FAIREST flower, no sooner blown but blasted,
Soft silken primrose fading timelessly,
Summer's chief honour, if thou hadst out-lasted
Bleak Winter's force that made thy blossom dry;
For he, being amorous on that lovely dye
   That did thy cheek envermeil, thought to kiss,
But killed, alas! and then bewailed his fatal bliss.

II

For since grim Aquilo, his charioteer,
By boisterous rape the Athenian damsel got,
He thought it touched his deity full near,
If likewise he some fair one wedded not;
Thereby to wipe away the infámous blot
   Of long-uncoupled bed and childless eld,
Which 'mongst the wanton gods a foul reproach was held.

THE DEATH OF A FAIR INFANT

III

So mounting up in icy-pearlèd car,
Through middle empire of the freezing air
He wandered long, till thee he spied from far;
There ended was his quest, there ceased his care.
Down he descended from his snow-soft chair,
  But all unwares, with his cold-kind embrace,
Unhoused thy virgin soul from her fair biding-place.

IV

Yet art thou not inglorious in thy fate;
For so Apollo, with unweeting hand,
Whilom did slay his dearly-lovèd mate,
Young Hyacinth born on Eurotas' strand,
Young Hyacinth the pride of Spartan land;
  But then transformed him to a purple flower;
Alack! that so to change thee Winter had no power!

V

Yet can I not persuade me thou art dead,
Or that thy corse corrupts in earth's dark womb,
Or that thy beauties lie in wormy bed,
Hid from the world in a low-delvèd tomb;
Could Heaven for pity thee so strictly doom?
  Oh no! for something in thy face did shine
Above mortality, that showed thou wast divine.

VI

Resolve me then, O Soul most surely blest
(If so it be that thou these plaints dost hear),
Tell me, bright Spirit, where'er thou hoverest
Whether above that high first-moving sphere,
Or in the Elysian fields (if such there were),
  Oh say me true if thou wert mortal wight,
And why from us so quickly thou didst take **thy flight.**

ON THE DEATH OF A FAIR INFANT

THE DEATH OF A FAIR INFANT

VII

Wert thou some star, which from the ruined roof
Of shaked Olympus by mischance didst fall;
Which careful Jove in nature's true behoof
Took up, and in fit place did reinstall?
Or did of late earth's sons besiege the wall
   Of sheeny Heaven, and thou some goddess fled
Amongst us here below to hide thy nectared head?

VIII

Or wert thou that just Maid who once before
Forsook the hated earth, oh tell me sooth,
And camest again to visit us once more?
Or wert thou [Mercy], that sweet-smiling Youth?
Or that crowned Matron, sage white-robèd Truth?
   Or any other of that heavenly brood
Let down in cloudy throne to do the world some good?

IX

Or wert thou of the golden-wingèd host,
Who having clad thyself in human weed,
To earth from thy prefixèd seat didst post,
And after short abode fly back with speed,
As if to show what creatures Heaven doth breed;
   Thereby to set the hearts of men on fire
To scorn the sordid world, and unto Heaven aspire?

X

But oh! why didst thou not stay here below
To bless us with thy heaven-loved innocence,
To slake his wrath whom sin hath made our foe,
To turn swift-rushing black perdition hence,
Or drive away the slaughtering pestilence,
   To stand 'twixt us and our deservèd smart?
But thou canst best perform that office where thou art.

THE DEATH OF A FAIR INFANT

Then thou, the mother of so sweet a child,
Her false-imagined loss cease to lament,
And wisely learn to curb thy sorrows wild ;
Think what a present thou to God hast sent,
And render him with patience what he lent ;
    This if thou do, he will an offspring give,
That till the world's last end shall make thy name to live.

AT A VACATION EXERCISE IN THE COLLEGE

*Part Latin, part English : the Latin Speeches ended,
the English thus began :*

HAIL, Native Language, that by sinews weak
Didst move my first endeavouring tongue to speak ;
And madest imperfect words with childish trips,
Half-unpronounced, slide through my infant lips,
Driving dumb Silence from the portal door,
Where he had mutely sat two years before ;
Here I salute thee, and thy pardon ask,
That now I use thee in my latter task.
Small loss it is that thence can come unto thee,
I know my tongue but little grace can do thee,
Thou need'st not be ambitious to be first,
Believe me I have thither packed the worst ;
And, if it happen as I did forecast,
The daintiest dishes shall be served up last.
I pray thee then deny me not thy aid
For this same small neglect that I have made ;
But haste thee straight to do me once a pleasure,
And from thy wardrobe bring thy chiefest treasure ;
Not those new-fangled toys, and trimming slight
Which takes our late fantastics with delight ;
But cull those richest robes and gayest attire,

AT A VACATION EXERCISE

Which deepest spirits and choicest wits desire.
I have some naked thoughts that rove about
And loudly knock to have their passage out ;
And weary of their place do only stay
Till thou hast decked them in thy best array ;
That so they may, without suspect or fears,
Fly swiftly to this fair assembly's ears.
Yet I had rather, if I were to choose,
Thy service in some graver subject use ;
Such as may make thee search thy coffers round,
Before thou clothe my fancy in fit sound ;
Such where the deep transported mind may soar
Above the wheeling poles, and at Heaven's door
Look in and see each blissful deity
How he before the thunderous throne doth lie,
Listening to what unshorn Apollo sings
To the touch of golden wires, while Hebè brings
Immortal nectar to her kingly sire ;
Then, passing through the spheres of watchful fire,
And misty regions of wide air next under,
And hills of snow and lofts of pilèd thunder,
May tell at length how green-eyed Neptune raves,
In Heaven's defiance mustering all his waves ;
Then sing of secret things that came to pass
When beldam Nature in her cradle was ;
And last of kings and queens and heroes old ;
Such as the wise Demodocus once told
In solemn songs at King Alcinous' feast,
While sad Ulysses' soul and all the rest
Are held with his melodious harmony
In willing chains and sweet captivity.
But fie, my wandering Muse how thou dost stray !
Expectance calls thee now another way,
Thou know'st it must be now thy only bent
To keep in compass of thy predicament.
Then quick about thy purposed business come,
That to the next I may resign my room.

AT A VACATION EXERCISE

Then ENS *is represented as father of the Predicaments, his ten
sons, whereof the eldest stood for* SUBSTANCE *with his canons;
which* ENS, *thus speaking, explains:*

Good luck befriend thee, Son ; for at thy birth
The faery ladies danced upon the hearth ;
Thy drowsy nurse hath sworn she did them spy
Come tripping to the room where thou didst lie,
And, sweetly singing round about thy bed,
Strew all their blessings on thy sleeping head.
She heard them give thee this, that thou shouldst still
From eyes of mortals walk invisible ;
Yet there is something that doth force my fear ;
For once it was my dismal hap to hear
A Sibyl old, bow-bent with crooked age,
That far events full wisely could presage,
And in Time's long and dark prospective glass
Foresaw what future days should bring to pass.
  "Your son," said she, "(nor can you it prevent)
Shall subject be to many an Accident.
O'er all his brethren he shall reign as king,
Yet every one shall make him underling,
And those that cannot live from him asunder
Ungratefully shall strive to keep him under ;
In worth and excellence he shall outgo them,
Yet, being above them, he shall be below them ;
From others he shall stand in need of nothing,
Yet on his brothers shall depend for clothing.
To find a foe it shall not be his hap,
And peace shall lull him in her flowery lap ;
Yet shall he live in strife, and at his door
Devouring war shall never cease to roar ;
Yea, it shall be his natural property
To harbour those that are at enmity."
What power, what force, what mighty spell, if not
Your learned hands, can loose this Gordian knot ?

8

AT A VACATION EXERCISE

The next, QUANTITY *and* QUALITY, *spake in prose, then* RELATION *was called by his name.*

Rivers, arise ; whether thou be the son
Of utmost Tweed, or Ouse, or gulfy Dun,
Or Trent, who, like some earth-born giant, spreads
His thirty arms along the indented meads ;
Or sullen Mole that runneth underneath,
Or Severn swift, guilty of maiden's death,
Or rocky Avon, or of sedgy Lea,
Or coaly Tyne, or ancient hallowed Dee,
Or Humber loud, that keeps the Scythian's name,
Or Medway smooth, or royal-towered Thame.

The rest was prose.

9

On the Morning of Christ's Nativity.

I

THIS is the month, and this the happy morn,
Wherein the Son of Heaven's eternal King,
Of wedded Maid, and Virgin Mother born,
Our great redemption from above did bring;
For so the holy sages once did sing,
    That he our deadly forfeit should release,
And with his Father work us a perpetual peace.

II

That glorious form, that light unsufferable,
And that far-beaming blaze of majesty,
Wherewith he wont at Heaven's high council-table

ON CHRIST'S NATIVITY

To sit the midst of Trinal Unity,
He laid aside; and, here with us to be,
   Forsook the courts of everlasting day,
And chose with us a darksome house of mortal clay.

III

Say, heavenly Muse, shall not thy sacred vein
Afford a present to the Infant God?
Hast thou no verse, no hymn, or solemn strain,
To welcome him to this his new abode,
Now, while the heaven, by the sun's team untrod,
   Hath took no print of the approaching light,
And all the spangled host keep watch in squadrons bright?

IV

See how from far upon the eastern road
The star-led wizards haste with odours sweet;
Oh! run, prevent them with thy humble ode,
And lay it lowly at his blessed feet;
Have thou the honour first thy Lord to greet,
   And join thy voice unto the angel quire,
From out his secret altar touched with hallowed fire.

THE HYMN

I

It was the winter wild,
While the Heaven-born child
   All meanly wrapped in the rude manger lies,
Nature in awe to him
Had doffed her gaudy trim,
   With her great Master so to sympathize;
It was no season then for her
To wanton with the Sun, her lusty paramour.

II

Only with speeches fair
She wooes the gentle air

ON CHRIST'S NATIVITY

To hide her guilty front with innocent snow,
And on her naked shame
Pollute with sinful blame,
 The saintly veil of maiden white to throw ;
Confounded, that her Maker's eyes
Should look so near upon her foul deformities.

III

But he, her fears to cease,
Sent down the meek-eyed Peace ;
 She, crowned with olive green, came softly sliding
Down through the turning sphere,
His ready harbinger,
 With turtle wing the amorous clouds dividing ;
And, waving wide her myrtle wand,
She strikes a universal peace through sea and land.

IV

No war, or battle's sound,
Was heard the world around ;
 The idle spear and shield were high up hung ;
The hookèd chariot stood
Unstained with hostile blood ;
 The trumpet spake not to the armed throng ;
And kings sat still with awful eye,
As if they surely knew their sovereign Lord was by.

V

But peaceful was the night
Wherein the Prince of Light
 His reign of peace upon the earth began ;
The winds, with wonder whist,
Smoothly the waters kissed,
 Whispering new joys to the mild ocean,
Who now hath quite forgot to rave,
While birds of calm sit brooding on the charmèd wave.

BUT HE, HER FEARS TO CEASE
SENT DOWN THE MEEK-EYED PEACE

VI

The stars, with deep amaze,
Stand fixed in steadfast gaze,
  Bending one way their precious influence,
And will not take their flight
For all the morning light,
  Or Lucifer that often warned them thence;
But in their glimmering orbs did glow,
Until their Lord himself bespake, and bid them go.

VII

And, though the shady gloom
Had given day her room,

15

ON CHRIST'S NATIVITY

The Sun himself withheld his wonted speed,
And hid his head for shame,
As his inferior flame
The new enlightened world no more should need;
He saw a greater Sun appear
Than his bright throne or burning axletree could bear.

VIII

The shepherds on the lawn,
Or ere the point of dawn,
  Sat simply chatting in a rustic row;
Full little thought they then,
That the mighty Pan
  Was kindly come to live with them below;
Perhaps their loves, or else their sheep,
Was all that did their silly thoughts so busy keep.

IX

When such music sweet
Their hearts and ears did greet,
  As never was by mortal finger strook;
Divinely-warbled voice
Answering the stringèd noise,
  As all their souls in blissful rapture took;
The air, such pleasure loth to lose,
With thousand echoes still prolongs each heavenly close.

X

Nature, that heard such sound,
Beneath the hollow round
  Of Cynthia's seat, the airy region thrilling,
Now was almost won
To think her part was done,
  And that her reign had here its last fulfilling;
She knew such harmony alone
Could hold all Heaven and Earth in happier union.

ON CHRIST'S NATIVITY

XI

At last surrounds their sight
A globe of circular light,
   That with long beams the shame-faced Night arrayed;
The helmèd Cherubim,
And sworded Seraphim,
   Are seen in glittering ranks with wings displayed,
Harping in loud and solemn quire,
With unexpressive notes, to Heaven's new-born Heir.

XII

Such music (as 'tis said)
Before was never made,
   But when of old the Sons of Morning sung,
While the Creator great
His constellations set,
   And the well-balanced world on hinges hung,
And cast the dark foundations deep,
And bid the weltering waves their oozy channel keep.

XIII

Ring out, ye crystal Spheres!
Once bless our human ears
   (If ye have power to touch our senses so),
And let your silver chime
Move in melodious time;
   And let the bass of Heaven's deep organ blow,
And with your ninefold harmony
Make up full consort to the angelic symphony.

XIV

For if such holy song
Enwrap our fancy long,
   Time will run back, and fetch the Age of Gold;
And speckled Vanity
Will sicken soon and die;
   And leprous Sin will melt from earthly mould;

ON CHRIST'S NATIVITY

And Hell itself will pass away,
And leave her dolorous mansions to the peering day.

XV

Yea, Truth and Justice then
Will down return to men,
   Orbed in a rainbow; and, like glories wearing,
Mercy will sit between,
Throned in celestial sheen,
   With radiant feet and tissued clouds down steering;
And, Heaven, as at some festival,
Will open wide the gates of her high palace hall.

XVI

But wisest Fate says No,
This must not yet be so,
   The Babe lies yet in smiling infancy,
That on the bitter cross
Must redeem our loss,
   So both himself and us to glorify;
Yet first, to those ychained in sleep,
The wakeful trump of doom must thunder through the deep,

XVII

With such a horrid clang
As on Mount Sinai rang,
   While the red fire and smouldering clouds outbrake;
The agèd earth, aghast
With terror of the blast,
   Shall from the surface to the centre shake;
When, at the world's last session,
The dreadful Judge in middle air shall spread his throne.

XVIII

And then at last our bliss
Full and perfect is,
   But now begins; for from this happy day
The old Dragon, under ground

18

ON CHRIST'S NATIVITY

In straiter limits bound,
  Not half so far casts his usurpèd sway,
And, wroth to see his kingdom fail,
Swindges the scaly horror of his folded tail.

XIX

The oracles are dumb,
No voice or hideous hum
  Runs through the archèd roof in words deceiving.
Apollo from his shrine
Can no more divine,
  With hollow shriek the steep of Delphos leaving.
No nightly trance, or breathèd spell,
Inspires the pale-eyed priest from the prophetic cell.

XX

The lonely mountains o'er
And the resounding shore,
  A voice of weeping heard and loud lament ;
From haunted spring and dale,
Edged with poplar pale,
  The parting Genius is with sighing sent ;
With flower-inwoven tresses torn
The Nymphs in twilight shade of tangled thickets mourn.

XXI

In consecrated earth,
And on the holy hearth,
  The Lars and Lemures moan with midnight plaint ;
In urns and altars round,
A drear and dying sound
  Affrights the Flamens at their service quaint ;
And the chill marble seems to sweat,
While each peculiar Power forgoes his wonted seat.

XXII

Peor and Baalim
Forsake their temples dim,

19

ON CHRIST'S NATIVITY

With that twice-battered god of Palestine ;
And moonèd Ashtaroth,
Heaven's queen and mother both,
   Now sits not girt with taper's holy shine ;
The Lybic Hammon shrinks his horn,
In vain the Tyrian maids their wounded Thammuz mourn.

XXIII

And sullen Moloch, fled,
Hath left in shadows dread
   His burning idol all of blackest hue ;
In vain, with cymbals' ring,
They call the grisly king,
   In dismal dance about the furnace blue ;
The brutish gods of Nile as fast,
Isis and Orus, and the dog Anubis, haste.

XXIV

Nor is Osiris seen
In Memphian grove or green,
   Trampling the unshowered grass with lowings loud ;
Nor can he be at rest
Within his sacred chest ;
   Nought but profoundest Hell can be his shroud !
In vain with timbreled anthems dark
The sable-stolèd sorcerers bear his worshipped ark.

XXV

He feels from Judah's land
The dreaded Infant's hand,
   The rays of Bethlehem blind his dusky eyn ;
Nor all the gods beside
Longer dare abide,
   Nor Typhon huge ending in snaky twine :
Our Babe, to show his Godhead true,
Can in His swaddling bands control the damnèd crew.

20

THE PARTING GENIUS IS WITH SIGHING SENT

ON CHRIST'S NATIVITY

So when the sun in bed,
Curtained with cloudy red,
   Pillows his chin upon an orient wave,
The flocking shadows pale
Troop to the infernal jail,
   Each fettered ghost slips to his several grave ;
And the yellow-skirted fays
Fly after the night-steeds, leaving their moon-loved maze.

XXVII

But see, the Virgin blest
Hath laid her Babe to rest ;
   Time is, our tedious song should here have ending ;
Heaven's youngest-teemèd star
Hath fixed her polished car,
   Her sleeping Lord with handmaid lamp attending ;
And all about the courtly stable
Bright-harnessed angels sit in order serviceable.

UPON THE CIRCUMCISION

YE flaming Powers, and wingèd Warriors bright,
That erst with music, and triumphant song,
First heard by happy watchful shepherds' ear,
So sweetly sung your joy the clouds along
Through the soft silence of the listening night,
Now mourn ; and, if sad share with us to bear
Your fiery essence can distil no tear,
Burn in your sighs, and borrow
Seas wept from our deep sorrow ;
He, who with all Heaven's heraldry whilere
Entered the world, now bleeds to give us ease ;
Alas, how soon our sin
   Sore doth begin
      His infancy to seize !

UPON THE CIRCUMCISION

Oh more exceeding love, or law more just?
Just law indeed, but more exceeding love!
For we, by rightful doom remediless,
Were lost in death, till He, that dwelt above
High throned in secret bliss, for us frail dust
Emptied his glory, even to nakedness;
And that great covenant which we still transgress
Entirely satisfied;
And the full wrath beside
Of vengeful justice bore for our excess;
And seals obedience first, with wounding smart,
This day; but oh, ere long,
   Huge pangs and strong
     Will pierce more near his heart.

THE PASSION

I

EREWHILE of music, and ethereal mirth,
Wherewith the stage of air and earth did ring,
And joyous news of Heavenly Infant's birth,
My Muse with Angels did divide to sing;
But headlong joy is ever on the wing,
   In wintry solstice like the shortened light
Soon swallowed up in dark, and long out-living night.

II

For now to sorrow must I tune my song,
And set my harp to notes of saddest woe,
Which on our dearest Lord did seize ere long,
Dangers, and snares, and wrongs, and worse than so,
Which he for us did freely undergo;
   Most perfect Hero, tried in heaviest plight
Of labours huge and hard, too hard for human wight!

III

He, sovereign Priest, stooping his regal head,
That dropped with odorous oil down his fair eyes,

THE PASSION

Poor fleshly tabernacle enterèd,
His starry front low-roofed beneath the skies;
Oh, what a mask was there, what a disguise!
  Yet more; the stroke of death he must abide,
Then lies him meekly down fast by his brethren's side.

IV

These latest scenes confine my roving verse;
To this horizon is my Phœbus bound.
His godlike acts, and his temptations fierce,
And former sufferings, otherwhere are found;
Loud o'er the rest Cremona's trump doth sound;
  Me softer airs befit, and softer strings
Of lute, or viol still, more apt for mournful things.

V

Befriend me, Night, best patroness of grief!
Over the pole thy thickest mantle throw,
And work my flattered fancy to belief
That heaven and earth are coloured with my woe;
My sorrows are too dark for day to know;
  The leaves should all be black whereon I write,
And letters, where my tears have washed, a wannish white.

VI

See, see the chariot, and those rushing wheels,
That whirled the prophet up at Chebar flood;
My spirit some transporting Cherub feels,
To bear me where the towers of Salem stood,
Once glorious towers, now sunk in guiltless blood.
  There doth my soul in holy vision sit,
In pensive trance, and anguish, and ecstatic fit.

VII

Mine eye hath found that sad sepulchral rock
That was the casket of Heaven's richest store;
And here though grief my feeble hands up lock,
Yet on the softened quarry would I score

25

THE PASSION

My plaining verse as lively as before ;
  For sure so well instructed are my tears,
That they would fitly fall in ordered characters.

VIII

Or should I, thence hurried on viewless wing,
Take up a weeping on the mountains wild,
The gentle neighbourhood of grove and spring
Would soon unbosom all their echoes mild ;
And I (for grief is easily beguiled)
  Might think the infection of my sorrows loud
Had got a race of mourners on some pregnant cloud.

*This subject the Author finding to be above the years he had
when he wrote it, and nothing satisfied with what was begun,
left it unfinished.*

ON SHAKESPEARE

1630

WHAT needs my Shakespeare for his honoured bones
The labour of an age in pilèd stones,
Or that his hallowed reliques should be hid
Under a star-ypointing pyramid ?
Dear son of memory, great heir of fame,
What need'st thou such weak witness of thy name ?
Thou in our wonder and astonishment
Hast built thyself a live-long monument.
For whilst to the shame of slow-endeavouring art
Thy easy numbers flow, and that each heart
Hath from the leaves of thy unvalued book
Those Delphic lines with deep impression took,
Then thou, our fancy of itself bereaving,
Dost make us marble with too much conceiving ;
And so sepúlchered in such pomp dost lie,
That kings for such a tomb would wish to die.

Song on May Morning.

Now the bright Morning-star, day's harbinger,
Comes dancing from the east, and leads with her
The flowery May, who from her green lap throws
The yellow cowslip and the pale primrose.
 Hail bounteous May, that dost inspire
 Mirth, and youth, and warm desire!
 Woods and groves are of thy dressing,
 Hill and dale doth boast thy blessing.
Thus we salute thee with our early song,
And welcome thee, and wish thee long.

ON THE UNIVERSITY CARRIER

Who sickened in the time of his vacancy, being forbid to go to London, by reason of the Plague

HERE lies old Hobson.   Death has broke his girt,
And here, alas! hath laid him in the dirt ;
Or else the ways being foul, twenty to one,
He's here stuck in a slough, and overthrown.
'Twas such a shifter, that (if truth were known)
Death was half glad when he had got him down ;
For he had any time this ten years full
Dodged with him betwixt Cambridge and The Bull.
And surely death could never have prevailed,
Had not his weekly course of carriage failed ;
But lately finding him so long at home,
And thinking now his journey's end was come,
And that he had ta'en up his latest inn,
In the kind office of a chamberlin
Showed him his room where he must lodge that night,
Pulled off his boots, and took away the light.
If any ask for him, it shall be said,
" Hobson has supped, and 's newly gone to bed."

ANOTHER ON THE SAME

HERE lieth one who did most truly prove
That he could never die while he could move ;
So hung his destiny, never to rot
While he might still jog on and keep his trot ;
Made of sphere-metal, never to decay
Until his revolution was at stay.
Time numbers motion, yet (without a crime
'Gainst old truth) motion numbered out his time ;
And, like an engine moved with wheel and weight,
His principles being ceased, he ended straight.
Rest, that gives all men life, gave him his death ;
And too much breathing put him out of breath ;
Nor were it contradiction to affirm
Too long vacation hastened on his term.
Merely to drive the time away he sickened,
Fainted, and died, nor would with ale be quickened.
" Nay," quoth he, on his swooning bed outstretched,
" If I mayn't carry, sure I'll ne'er be fetched ;
But vow, though the cross doctors all stood hearers,
For one carrier put down to make six bearers."
Ease was his chief disease, and, to judge right,
He died for heaviness that his cart went light.
His leisure told him that his time was come,
And lack of load made his life burdensome,
That even to his last breath (there be that say't)
As he were pressed to death, he cried, " More weight ! "
But, had his doings lasted as they were,
He had been an immortal carrier.
Obedient to the moon he spent his date
In course reciprocal, and had his fate
Linked to the mutual flowing of the seas,
Yet (strange to think) his wain was his increase.
His letters are delivered all and gone,
Only remains this superscription.

AN EPITAPH

ON THE MARCHIONESS OF WINCHESTER

THIS rich marble doth inter
The honoured wife of Winchester,
A Viscount's daughter, an Earl's heir,
Besides what her virtues fair
Added to her noble birth,
More than she could own from earth.
Summers three times eight save one
She had told : alas ! too soon,
After so short time of breath,
To house with darkness, and with death !
Yet, had the number of her days
Been as complete as was her praise,
Nature and Fate had had no strife
In giving limit to her life.
Her high birth, and her graces sweet,
Quickly found a lover meet ;
The virgin quire for her request
The god that sits at marriage feast ;
He at their invoking came,
But with a scarce well-lighted flame ;
And in his garland, as he stood,
Ye might discern a cypress bud.
Once had the early matrons run
To greet her of a lovely son ;
And now with second hope she goes,
And calls Lucina to her throes ;
But, whether by mischance or blame,
Atropos for Lucina came ;
And, with remorseless cruelty,
Spoiled at once both fruit and tree.
The hapless babe before his birth
Had burial, not yet laid in earth ;
And the languished mother's womb
Was not long a living tomb.
So have I seen some tender slip,
Saved with care from winter's nip,

AN EPITAPH

The pride of her carnation train,
Plucked up by some unheedy swain,
Who only thought to crop the flower
New shot up from vernal shower;
But the fair blossom hangs the head
Sideways, as on a dying bed,
And those pearls of dew she wears,
Prove to be presaging tears,
Which the sad morn had let fall
On her hastening funeral.
Gentle Lady, may thy grave
Peace and quiet ever have!
After this thy travail sore,
Sweet rest seize thee evermore,
That, to give the world increase,
Shortened hast thy own life's lease!
Here, besides the sorrowing
That thy noble house doth bring,
Here be tears of perfect moan
Wept for thee in Helicon;
And some flowers and some bays
For thy hearse, to strew the ways,
Sent thee from the banks of Came,
Devoted to thy virtuous name;
Whilst thou, bright Saint, high sitt'st in glory,
Next her, much like to thee in story,
That fair Syrian shepherdess,
Who, after years of barrenness,
The highly-favoured Joseph bore
To him that served for her before,
And at her next birth, much like thee,
Through pangs fled to felicity,
Far within the bosom bright
Of blazing Majesty and Light;
There with thee, new-welcome Saint,
Like fortunes may her soul acquaint,
With thee there clad in radiant sheen,
No Marchioness, but now a Queen.

ON TIME.

(To be set on a clock-case)

FLY, envious Time, till thou run out thy race;
Call on the lazy, leaden-stepping Hours,
Whose speed is but the heavy plummet's pace;
And glut thyself with what thy womb devours,
Which is no more than what is false and vain,
And merely mortal dross;
So little is our loss,
So little is thy gain!
For, whenas each thing bad thou hast entombed,
And last of all thy greedy self consumed,
Then long Eternity shall greet our bliss
With an individual kiss;
And Joy shall overtake us as a flood,
When everything that is sincerely good
And perfectly divine,

32

With Truth, and Peace, and Love, shall ever shine
About the supreme throne
Of Him, to whose happy-making sight alone
When once our heavenly-guided soul shall climb,
Then, all this earthly grossness quit,
Attired with stars, we shall for ever sit,
    Triumphing over Death, and Chance, and thee, O Time

At a Solemn Music.

BLEST pair of Sirens, pledges of Heaven's joy,
Sphere-born harmonious sisters, Voice and Verse,
Wed your divine sounds, and mixed power employ,
Dead things with inbreathed sense able to pierce;
And to our high-raised phantasy present
That undisturbèd song of pure concent,
Aye sung before the sapphire-coloured throne,
To Him that sits thereon,

AT A SOLEMN MUSIC

With saintly shout, and solemn jubilee ;
Where the bright Seraphim, in burning row,
Their loud uplifted angel-trumpets blow ;
And the Cherubic host, in thousand choirs,
Touch their immortal harps of golden wires,
With those just Spirits that wear victorious palms,
Hymns devout and holy psalms
Singing everlastingly ;
That we on earth, with undiscording voice,
May rightly answer that melodious noise ;
As once we did, till disproportioned sin
Jarred against Nature's chime, and with harsh din
Broke the fair music that all creatures made
To their great Lord, whose love their motion swayed
In perfect diapason, whilst they stood
In first obedience, and their state of good.
Oh, may we soon again renew that song,
And keep in tune with Heaven, till God, ere long,
To his celestial consort us unite,
To live with Him, and sing in endless morn of light !

LAUGHTER HOLDING BOTH HIS SIDES

L'ALLEGRO.

Hence, loathed Melancholy,
Of Cerberus and blackest Midnight born,
   In Stygian cave forlorn,
'Mongst horrid shapes, and shrieks, and sights unholy!
Find out some uncouth cell,
   Where brooding Darkness spreads his jealous wings,
And the night-raven sings;
   There, under ebon shades and low-browed rocks,
As rugged as thy locks,
   In dark Cimmerian desert ever dwell.
But come, thou Goddess fair and free,
In heaven yclept Euphrosyne,

L'ALLEGRO

And by men, heart-easing Mirth :
Whom lovely Venus, at a birth,
With two sister Graces more,
To ivy-crowned Bacchus bore ;
Or whether (as some sager sing)
The frolic wind that breathes the spring,
Zephyr, with Aurora playing,
As he met her once a-Maying ;
There, on beds of violets blue,
And fresh-blown roses washed in dew,
Filled her with thee, a daughter fair,
So buxom, blithe, and debonair.
Haste thee, Nymph, and bring with thee
Jest and youthful Jollity,
Quips and Cranks, and wanton Wiles,
Nods, and Becks, and wreathèd Smiles,
Such as hang on Hebe's cheek,
And love to live in dimple sleek ;
Sport, that wrinkled Care derides,
And Laughter holding both his sides.
Come, and trip it, as you go,
On the light fantastic toe ;
And in thy right hand lead with thee
The mountain nymph, sweet Liberty ;
And, if I give thee honour due,
Mirth, admit me of thy crew,
To live with her and live with thee,
In unreproved pleasures free ;
To hear the lark begin his flight,
And singing, startle the dull night,
From his watch-tower in the skies,
Till the dappled dawn doth rise ;
Then to come, in spite of sorrow,
And at my window bid good-morrow,
Through the sweet-briar, or the vine,
Or the twisted eglantine ;
While the cock, with lively din,

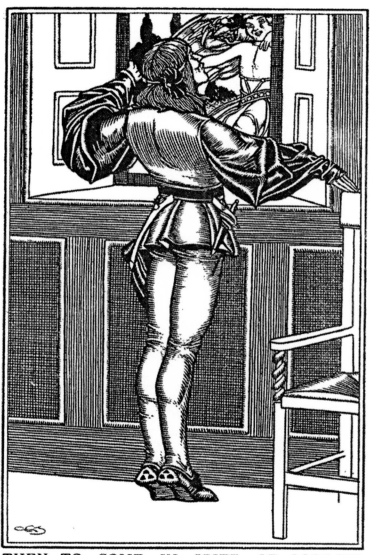

THEN TO COME, IN SPITE OF SORROW,
AND AT MY WINDOW BID GOOD-MORROW

L'ALLEGRO

Scatters the rear of darkness thin,
And to the stack, or the barn-door,
Stoutly struts his dames before ;
Oft listening how the hounds and horn
Cheerly rouse the slumbering morn,
From the side of some hoar hill,
Through the high wood echoing shrill :
Sometime walking, not unseen,
By hedgerow elms, on hillocks green,
Right against the eastern gate,
Where the great Sun begins his state,
Robed in flames and amber light,
The clouds in thousand liveries dight ;
Whilst the ploughman, near at hand,

L'ALLEGRO

Whistles o'er the furrowed land,
And the milkmaid singeth blithe,
And the mower whets his scythe,
And every shepherd tells his tale
Under the hawthorn in the dale.
Straight mine eye hath caught new pleasures,
Whilst the landscape round it measures ;
Russet lawns and fallows gray,
Where the nibbling flocks do stray,
Mountains on whose barren breast
The labouring clouds do often rest ;
Meadows trim, with daisies pied ;
Shallow brooks, and rivers wide ;
Towers and battlements it sees
Bosomed high in tufted trees,
Where perhaps some beauty lies,
The cynosure of neighbouring eyes.
Hard-by, a cottage chimney smokes
From betwixt two aged oaks,
Where Corydon and Thyrsis met
Are at their savoury dinner set
Of herbs and other country messes,
Which the neat-handed Phyllis dresses ;
And then in haste her bower she leaves,
With Thestylis to bind the sheaves ;
Or if the earlier season lead,
To the tanned haycock in the mead.
Sometimes, with secure delight,
The upland hamlets will invite,
When the merry bells ring round,
And the jocund rebecks sound
To many a youth, and many a maid,
Dancing in the chequered shade ;
And young and old come forth to play
On a sunshine holiday,
Till the livelong daylight fail ;
Then to the spicy nut-brown ale,

SHE WAS PINCHED AND PULLED, SHE SAID;
AND HE, BY FRIAR'S LANTERN LED

L'ALLEGRO

With stories told of many a feat,
How Fairy Mab the junkets eat ;
She was pinched and pulled, she said ;
And he, by Friar's lantern led,
Tells how the drudging goblin sweat,
To earn his cream-bowl duly set,
When in one night, ere glimpse of morn,
His shadowy flail hath threshed the corn
That ten day-labourers could not end ;
Then lies him down the lubber fiend,
And, stretched out all the chimney's length,
Basks at the fire his hairy strength,
And crop-full out of doors he flings,
Ere the first cock his matin rings.
Thus done the tales, to bed they creep,
By whispering winds soon lulled asleep.
Towered cities please us then,
And the busy hum of men,
Where throngs of knights and barons bold
In weeds of peace high triumphs hold,
With store of ladies, whose bright eyes
Rain influence, and judge the prize
Of wit or arms, while both contend
To win her grace whom all commend.
There let Hymen oft appear,
In saffron robe, with taper clear,
And pomp, and feast, and revelry,
With mask and antique pageantry ;
Such sights as youthful poets dream
On summer eves by haunted stream.
Then to the well-trod stage anon,
If Jonson's learned sock be on,
Or sweetest Shakespeare, Fancy's child,
Warble his native wood-notes wild,
And ever, against eating cares,
Lap me in soft Lydian airs,
Married to immortal verse,

Such as the meeting soul may pierce,
In notes with many a winding bout
Of linked sweetness long drawn out,
With wanton heed, and giddy cunning,
The melting voice through mazes running,
Untwisting all the chains that tie
The hidden soul of harmony ;
That Orpheus' self may heave his head

SUCH SIGHTS AS YOUTHFUL POETS DREAM
ON SUMMER EVES BY HAUNTED STREAM

From golden slumber on a bed
Of heaped Elysian flowers, and hear
Such strains as would have won the ear
Of Pluto, to have quite set free
His half-regained Eurydice.
    These delights, if thou canst give,
Mirth, with thee I mean to live.

IL PENSEROSO.

HENCE, vain deluding Joys,
The brood of Folly without father bred!
  How little you bested,
Or fill the fixed mind with all your toys!
  Dwell in some idle brain,
And fancies fond with gaudy shapes possess,
  As thick and numberless
As the gay motes that people the sunbeams,
  Or likest hovering dreams,
The fickle pensioners of Morpheus' train.
  But hail, thou Goddess, sage and holy!
Hail, divinest Melancholy!
Whose saintly visage is too bright
To hit the sense of human sight,
And therefore to our weaker view
O'erlaid with black, staid Wisdom's hue;
Black, but such as in esteem
Prince Memnon's sister might beseem,
Or that starred Ethiop queen that strove
To set her beauty's praise above
The Sea-nymphs, and their powers offended.
Yet thou art higher far descended;
Thee bright-haired Vesta long of yore
To solitary Saturn bore;
His daughter she; in Saturn's reign,
Such mixture was not held a stain.

MELANCHOLY

IL PENSEROSO

Oft in glimmering bowers and glades
He met her, and in secret shades
Of woody Ida's inmost grove,
While yet there was no fear of Jove.
Come, pensive Nun, devout and pure,
Sober, steadfast, and demure,
All in a robe of darkest grain,

IL PENSEROSO

Flowing with majestic train,
And sable stole of cypress lawn,
Over thy decent shoulders drawn.
Come, but keep thy wonted state,
With even step, and musing gait,
And looks commercing with the skies,
Thy rapt soul sitting in thine eyes;
There, held in holy passion still,
Forget thyself to marble, till,
With a sad leaden downward cast,
Thou fix them on the earth as fast.
And join with the calm Peace and Quiet,
Spare Fast, that oft with gods doth diet,
And hears the Muses in a ring
Aye round about Jove's altar sing;
And add to these retired Leisure,
That in trim gardens takes his pleasure;
But, first and chiefest, with thee bring
Him that yon soars on golden wing,
Guiding the fiery-wheeled throne,
The Cherub Contemplation;
And the mute Silence hist along,
'Less Philomel will deign a song,
In her sweetest saddest plight,
Smoothing the rugged brow of Night,
While Cynthia checks her dragon yoke
Gently o'er the accustomed oak.
Sweet bird, that shunn'st the noise of folly,
Most musical, most melancholy!
Thee, chauntress, oft the woods among
I woo, to hear thy evensong;
And missing thee, I walk unseen
On the dry smooth-shaven green,
To behold the wandering moon,
Riding near her highest noon,
Like one that had been led astray
Through the heaven's wide pathless way,

IL PENSEROSO

And oft, as if her head she bowed,
Stooping through a fleecy cloud.
Oft on a plat of rising ground,
I hear the far-off curfew sound,
Over some wide-watered shore,
Swinging slow with sullen roar ;
Or, if the air will not permit,
Some still removed place will fit,
Where glowing embers through the room
Teach light to counterfeit a gloom,
Far from all resort of mirth,
Save the cricket on the hearth,

Or the bellman's drowsy charm
To bless the doors from nightly harm;
Or let my lamp, at midnight hour,
Be seen in some high lonely tower,
Where I may oft outwatch the Bear,
With thrice-great Hermes, or unsphere
The spirit of Plato, to unfold
What worlds, or what vast regions hold
The immortal mind that hath forsook
Her mansion in this fleshly nook;
And of those demons that are found

SUCH NOTES, AS, WARBLED TO THE STRING,
DREW IRON TEARS DOWN PLUTO'S CHEEK

IL PENSEROSO

In fire, air, flood, or underground,
Whose power hath a true consent
With planet, or with element.
Sometime let gorgeous Tragedy
In sceptered pall come sweeping by,
Presenting Thebes, or Pelops' line,
Or the tale of Troy divine,
Or what (though rare) of later age
Ennobled hath the buskined stage.
But, O sad Virgin ! that thy power
Might raise Musæus from his bower.
Or bid the soul of Orpheus sing
Such notes, as, warbled to the string,
Drew iron tears down Pluto's cheek,
And made Hell grant what love did seek ;
Or call up him that left half-told
The story of Cambuscan bold,
Of Camball, and of Algarsife,
And who had Canace to wife,
That owned the virtuous ring and glass,
And of the wondrous horse of brass
On which the Tartar king did ride :
And if aught else great bards beside
In sage and solemn tunes have sung,
Of tourneys, and of trophies hung,
Of forests, and enchantments drear,
Where more is meant than meets the ear.
Thus, Night, oft see me in thy pale career,
Till civil-suited Morn appear,
Not tricked and frounced, as she was wont
With the Attic boy to hunt,
But kerchiefed in a comely cloud,
While rocking winds are piping loud ;
Or ushered with a shower still,
When the gust hath blown his fill,
Ending on the rustling leaves,
With minute-drops from off the eaves.

IL PENSEROSO

And, when the sun begins to fling
His flaring beams, me, Goddess, bring
To arched walks of twilight groves,
And shadows brown, that Sylvan loves,
Of pine, or monumental oak,
Where the rude axe with heaved stroke
Was never heard the Nymphs to daunt,
Or fright them from their hallowed haunt.
There in close covert by some brook,
Where no profaner eye may look,
Hide me from day's garish eye,
While the bee with honeyed thigh,
That at her flowery work doth sing,

THERE IN CLOSE COVERT BY SOME BROOK,
WHERE NO PROFANER EYE MAY LOOK

IL PENSEROSO

And the waters murmuring,
With such consort as they keep,
Entice the dewy-feathered Sleep;
And let some strange mysterious dream
Wave at his wings, in airy stream
Of lively portraiture displayed,

63

IL PENSEROSO

Softly on my eyelids laid.
And, as I wake, sweet music breathe
Above, about, or underneath,
Sent by some Spirit to mortals good,
Or the unseen Genius of the wood.
But let my due feet never fail
To walk the studious cloister's pale,
And love the high embowed roof,
With antique pillars massy proof,
And storied windows richly dight,
Casting a dim religious light.
There let the pealing organ blow,
To the full-voiced quire below,
In service high and anthems clear,
As may with sweetness, through mine ear,
Dissolve me into ecstasies,
And bring all Heaven before mine eyes.
And may at last my weary age
Find out the peaceful hermitage,
The hairy gown and mossy cell,
Where I may sit and rightly spell
Of every star that heaven doth shew,
And every herb that sips the dew ;
Till old experience do attain
To something like prophetic strain.
These pleasures, Melancholy, give,
And I with thee will choose to live.

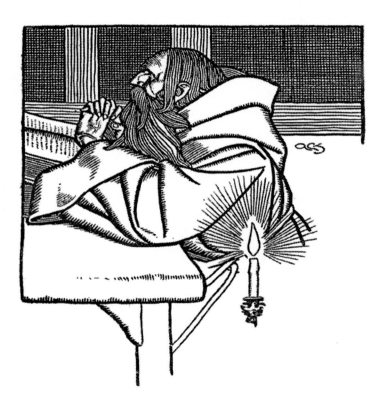

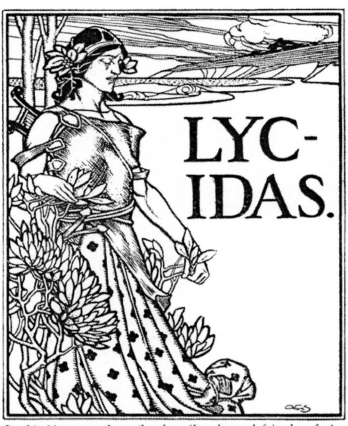

LYC-IDAS.

In this MONODY *the author bewails a learned friend, unfortu-*
nately drowned in his passage from Chester on the Irish seas,
1637; and by occasion foretells the ruin of our corrupted
clergy, then in their height.

YET once more, O ye laurels, and once more,
Ye myrtles brown, with ivy never sere,
I come to pluck your berries harsh and crude,
And with forced fingers rude
Shatter your leaves before the mellowing year.
Bitter constraint, and sad occasion dear

66

WHERE WERE YE, NYMPHS, WHEN THE REMORSELESS DEEP
CLOSED O'ER THE HEAD OF YOUR LOVED LYCIDAS?

LYCIDAS

Compels me to disturb your season due ;
For Lycidas is dead, dead ere his prime,
Young Lycidas, and hath not left his peer.
Who would not sing for Lycidas? he knew
Himself to sing, and build the lofty rhyme.
He must not float upon his watery bier
Unwept, and welter to the parching wind,
Without the meed of some melodious tear.
   Begin then, Sisters of the sacred well
That from beneath the seat of Jove doth spring ;
Begin, and somewhat loudly sweep the string.
Hence with denial vain, and coy excuse ;
So may some gentle Muse
With lucky words favour my destined urn ;
And as he passes turn,
And bid fair peace be to my sable shroud.
For we were nursed upon the self-same hill,
Fed the same flock, by fountain, shade, and rill.
Together both, ere the high lawns appeared
Under the opening eyelids of the morn,
We drove afield, and both together heard
What time the gray-fly winds her sultry horn
Battening our flocks with the fresh dews of night,
Oft till the star that rose at evening, bright,
Toward Heaven's descent had sloped his westering wheel.
Meanwhile the rural ditties were not mute,
Tempered to the oaten flute ;
Rough Satyrs danced, and Fauns with cloven heel
From the glad sound would not be absent long,
And old Damœtas loved to hear our song.
   But oh, the heavy change, now thou art gone,
Now thou art gone, and never must return !
Thee, shepherd, thee the woods, and desert caves,
With wild thyme and the gadding vine o'ergrown,
And all their echoes mourn.
The willows, and the hazel copses green,
Shall now no more be seen ·

LYCIDAS

Fanning their joyous leaves to thy soft lays.
As killing as the canker to the rose,
Or taint-worm to the weanling herds that graze,
Or frost to flowers, that their gay wardrobe wear,
When first the white-thorn blows ;
Such Lycidas, thy loss to shepherd's ear.

    Where were ye, Nymphs, when the remorseless deep
Closed o'er the head of your loved Lycidas ?
For neither were ye playing on the steep,
Where your old bards, the famous Druids, lie,
Nor on the shaggy top of Mona high,
Nor yet where Deva spreads her wizard stream.
Ay me, I fondly dream !
Had ye been there, for what could that have done ?
What could the Muse herself that Orpheus bore,
The Muse herself, for her enchanting son
Whom universal Nature did lament,
When, by the rout that made the hideous roar,
His gory visage down the stream was sent,
Down the swift Hebrus to the Lesbian shore ?

   Alas ! what boots it with incessant care
To tend the homely slighted shepherd's trade,
And strictly meditate the thankless Muse ?
Were it not better done, as others use,
To sport with Amaryllis in the shade,
Or with the tangles of Neæra's hair ?
Fame is the spur that the clear spirit doth raise
(That last infirmity of noble mind)
To scorn delights, and live laborious days ;
But the fair guerdon when we hope to find,
And think to burst out into sudden blaze,
Comes the blind Fury with the abhorred shears,
And slits the thin-spun life. 'But not the praise,'
Phœbus replied, and touched my trembling ears :
'Fame is no plant that grows on mortal soil,
Nor in the glistening foil
Set off to the world, nor in broad rumour lies.

But lives and spreads aloft by those pure eyes
And perfect witness of all-judging Jove ;
As he pronounces lastly on each deed,
Of so much fame in Heaven expect thy meed.'
    Of fountain Arethuse, and thou honoured flood,
Smooth-sliding Mincius, crowned with vocal reeds,
That strain I heard was of a higher mood.
But now my oat proceeds,
And listens to the herald of the sea,
That came in Neptune's plea ;

LYCIDAS

He asked the waves, and asked the felon winds,
What hard mishap hath doomed this gentle swain?
And questioned every gust of rugged wings
That blows from off each beaked promontory.
They knew not of his story;
And sage Hippotades their answer brings,
That not a blast was from his dungeon strayed;
The air was calm, and on the level brine
Sleek Panope with all her sisters played.
It was that fatal and perfidious bark,
Built in the eclipse, and rigged with curses dark,
That sunk so low that sacred head of thine.
    Next Camus, reverend sire, went footing slow,
His mantle hairy, and his bonnet sedge,
Inwrought with figures dim, and on the edge,
Like to that sanguine flower inscribed with woe.
'Ah! who hath reft,' quoth he, 'my dearest pledge?'
Last came and last did go,
The pilot of the Galilean lake;
Two massy keys he bore, of metals twain
(The golden opes, the iron shuts amain).
He shook his mitred locks, and stern bespake:
'How well could I have spared for thee, young swain,
Enow of such as for their bellies' sake
Creep, and intrude, and climb into the fold!
Of other care they little reckoning make,
Than how to scramble at the shearers' feast,
And shove away the worthy bidden guest.
Blind mouths! that scarce themselves know how to hold
A sheephook, or have learned aught else the least
That to the faithful herdsman's art belongs!
What recks it them? What need they? They are sped;
And, when they list, their lean and flashy songs
Grate on their scrannel pipes of wretched straw;
The hungry sheep look up, and are not fed,
But swoln with wind and the rank mist they draw,
Rot inwardly, and foul contagion spread;

LYCIDAS

Besides what the grim wolf with privy paw
Daily devours apace, and nothing said.
But that two-handed engine at the door
Stands ready to smite once, and smite no more.'
    Return, Alpheus, the dread voice is past
That shrunk thy streams ; return, Sicilian Muse,
And call the vales, and bid them hither cast
Their bells, and flowerets of a thousand hues.
Ye valleys low, where the mild whispers use
Of shades, and wanton winds, and gushing brooks,
On whose fresh lap the swart star sparely looks,
Throw hither all your quaint enamelled eyes,
That on the green turf suck the honied showers,
And purple all the ground with vernal flowers.
Bring the rathe primrose that forsaken dies,
The tufted crow-toe and pale jessamine,
The white pink, and the pansy freaked with jet,
The glowing violet,
The musk-rose, and the well-attired woodbine,
With cowslips wan that hang the pensive head,
And every flower that sad embroidery wears :
Bid Amaranthus all his beauty shed,
And daffadillies fill their cups with tears,
To strew the laureate hearse where Lycid lies.
For so, to interpose a little ease,
Let our frail thoughts dally with false surmise.
Ay me ! whilst thee the shores and sounding seas
Wash far away, where'er thy bones are hurled ;
Whether beyond the stormy Hebrides,
Where thou perhaps under the whelming tide,
Visit'st the bottom of the monstrous world ;
Or whether thou, to our moist vows denied,
Sleep'st by the fable of Bellerus old,
Where the great Vision of the guarded Mount
Looks toward Namancos and Bayona's hold ;
Look homeward, Angel, now, and melt with ruth ;
And, O ye dolphins, waft the hapless youth.

LYCIDAS

    Weep no more, woeful shepherds, weep no more,
For Lycidas your sorrow is not dead,
Sunk though he be beneath the watery floor.
So sinks the day-star in the ocean bed,
And yet anon repairs his drooping head,
And tricks his beams, and with new-spangled ore
Flames in the forehead of the morning sky:
So Lycidas sunk low, but mounted high,
Through the dear might of Him that walked the waves,
Where, other groves and other streams along,
With nectar pure his oozy locks he laves;
And hears the unexpressive nuptial song,
In the blest kingdoms meek of joy and love.
There entertain him all the Saints above,
In solemn troops, and sweet societies,
That sing, and singing in their glory move,
And wipe the tears for ever from his eyes.
Now, Lycidas, the shepherds weep no more:
Henceforth thou art the Genius of the shore,
In thy large recompense, and shalt be good
To all that wander in that perilous flood.

    Thus sang the uncouth swain to the oaks and rills,
While the still morn went out with sandals gray;

LYCIDAS

He touched the tender tops of various quills,
With eager thought warbling his Doric lay.
And now the sun had stretched out all the hills,
And now was dropped into the western bay ;
At last he rose, and twitched his mantle blue ;
To-morrow to fresh woods, and pastures new.

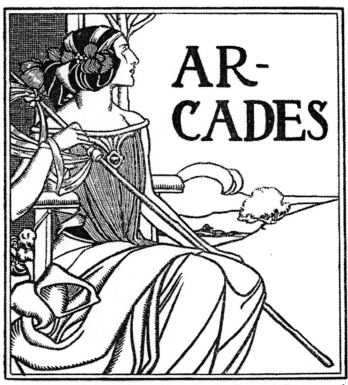

AR-CADES

Part of an Entertainment presented to the Countess Dowager of Derby at Harefield, by some noble persons of her family, who appear on the scene in pastoral habit, moving toward the seat of state, with this Song.

Song I

LOOK nymphs, and shepherds look!
What sudden blaze of majesty
Is that which we from hence descry,
Too divine to be mistook?
   This, this is she,
To whom our vows and wishes bend;
Here our solemn search hath end.

76

ARCADES

Fame, that her high worth to raise
Seemed erst so lavish and profuse,
We may justly now accuse
Of detraction from her praise ;
   Less than half we find expressed,
   Envy bid conceal the rest.

Mark what radiant state she spreads,
In circle round her shining throne ;
Shooting her beams like silver threads ;
This, this is she alone,
   Sitting like a goddess bright,
   In the centre of her light.

Might she the wise Latona be,
Or the towered Cybele,
Mother of a hundred gods ?
Juno dares not give her odds ;
   Who had thought this clime had held
   A deity so unparalleled ?

As they come forward, THE GENIUS OF THE WOOD
appears, and turning towards them, speaks.

GENIUS

   Stay, gentle swains, for, though in this disguise,
I see bright honour sparkle through your eyes ;
Of famous Arcady ye are, and sprung
Of that renownèd flood, so often sung,
Divine Alpheus, who by secret sluice
Stole under seas to meet his Arethuse ;
And ye, the breathing roses of the wood,
Fair silver-buskined Nymphs as great and good ;
I know this quest of yours, and free intent
Was all in honour and devotion meant
To the great mistress of yon princely shrine,
Whom with low reverence I adore as mine,
And with all helpful service will comply

ARCADES

To further this night's glad solemnity;
And lead ye where ye may more near behold
What shallow-searching Fame hath left untold;
Which I full oft, amidst these shades alone,
Have sat to wonder at, and gaze upon.
For know, by lot from Jove I am the Power
Of this fair wood, and live in oaken bower,
To nurse the saplings tall, and curl the grove
With ringlets quaint, and wanton windings wove.
And all my plants I save from nightly ill
Of noisome winds and blasting vapours chill;
And from the boughs brush off the evil dew,
And heal the harms of thwarting thunder blue,
Or what the cross dire-looking planet smites,
Or hurtful worm with cankered venom bites.
When evening gray doth rise, I fetch my round
Over the mount, and all this hallowed ground;
And early ere the odorous breath of morn
Awakes the slumbering leaves, or tasselled horn
Shakes the high thicket, haste I all about,
Number my ranks, and visit every sprout
With puissant words, and murmurs made to bless.
But else in deep of night, when drowsiness
Hath locked up mortal sense, then listen I
To the celestial Sirens' harmony,
That sit upon the nine enfolded spheres,
And sing to those that hold the vital shears,
And turn the adamantine spindle round,
On which the fate of gods and men is wound.
Such sweet compulsion doth in music lie,
To lull the daughters of Necessity,
And keep unsteady Nature to her law,
And the low world in measured motion draw
After the heavenly tune, which none can hear
Of human mould with gross unpurgèd ear;
And yet such music worthiest were to blaze
The peerless height of her immortal praise

THE GENIUS OF THE WOOD APPEARS

ARCADES

Whose lustre leads us, and for her most fit,
If my inferior hand or voice could hit
Inimitable sounds ; yet as we go,
Whate'er the skill of lesser gods can show
I will assay, her worth to celebrate ;
And so attend ye toward her glittering state ;
Where ye may all that are of noble stem,
Approach, and kiss her sacred vesture's hem.

Song II

O'er the smooth enamelled green,
Where no print of step hath been,
    Follow me, as I sing
    And touch the warbled string.
Under the shady roof
Of branching elm star-proof,
    Follow me.
I will bring you where she sits,
Clad in splendour as befits
    Her deity.
Such a rural Queen
All Arcadia hath not seen.

Song III

Nymphs and shepherds dance no more
    By sandy Ladon's lilied banks ;
On old Lycæus, or Cyllene hoar,
    Trip no more in twilight ranks ;
Though Erymanth your loss deplore,
    A better soil shall give ye thanks.

From the stony Mænalus
Bring your flocks, and live with us ;
Here ye shall have greater grace,
To serve the Lady of this place.
Though Syrinx your Pan's mistress were,
Yet Syrinx well might wait on her.
    Such a rural Queen
    All Arcadia hath not seen.

COMUS

THE PERSONS

THE ATTENDANT SPIRIT, *afterwards in the habit of* THYRSIS.
COMUS, *with his Crew.*
THE LADY.
FIRST BROTHER.
SECOND BROTHER.
SABRINA, *the Nymph.*

THE CHIEF PERSONS WHICH PRESENTED WERE:

The Lord BRACKLEY.
Mr. THOMAS EGERTON, *his brother.*
The Lady ALICE EGERTON.

THE ATTENDANT SPIRIT

The first Scene discovers a wild wood.

The ATTENDANT SPIRIT *descends or enters.*

BEFORE the starry threshold of Jove's court
My mansion is, where those immortal shapes
Of bright aërial spirits live insphered
In regions mild of calm and serene air,
Above the smoke and stir of this dim spot,
Which men call earth, and, with low-thoughted care,
Confined and pestered in this pinfold here,
Strive to keep up a frail and feverish being ;

85

COMUS

Unmindful of the crown that Virtue gives,
After this mortal change, to her true servants
Amongst the enthroned gods on sainted seats.
Yet some there be that by due steps aspire
To lay their just hands on that golden key
That opes the palace of eternity ;
To such my errand is ; and, but for such,
I would not soil these pure ambrosial weeds
With the rank vapours of this sin-worn mould.
But to my task. Neptune, besides the sway
Of every salt flood and each ebbing stream,
Took in, by lot 'twixt high and nether Jove,
Imperial rule of all the sea-girt isles,
That, like to rich and various gems, inlay
The unadorned bosom of the deep ;
Which he, to grace his tributary gods,
By course commits to several government,
And gives them leave to wear their sapphire crowns,
And wield their little tridents.   But this Isle,
The greatest and the best of all the main,
He quarters to his blue-haired deities ;
And all this tract that fronts the falling sun,
A noble Peer of mickle trust and power
Has in his charge, with tempered awe to guide
An old and haughty nation, proud in arms ;
Where his fair offspring, nursed in princely lore,
Are coming to attend their father's state,
And new-entrusted sceptre.   But their way
Lies through the perplexed paths of this drear wood,
The nodding horror of whose shady brows
Threats the forlorn and wandering passenger ;
And here their tender age might suffer peril,
But that by quick command from sovran Jove,
I was despatched for their defence and guard.
And listen why ; for I will tell you now
What never yet was heard in tale or song,
From old or modern bard, in hall or bower.

COMUS

Bacchus, that first from out the purple grape
Crushed the sweet poison of misused wine,
After the Tuscan mariners transformed,
Coasting the Tyrrhene shore, as the winds listed,
On Circe's island fell. (Who knows not Circe,
The daughter of the Sun, whose charmed cup
Whoever tasted lost his upright shape,
And downward fell into a grovelling swine?)
This Nymph that gazed upon his clustering locks,
With ivy berries wreathed, and his blithe youth,
Had by him, ere he parted thence, a son
Much like his father, but his mother more,
Whom therefore she brought up and Comus named;
Who, ripe and frolic of his full-grown age,
Roving the Celtic and Iberian fields,
At last betakes him to this ominous wood,
And in thick shelter of black shades embowered,
Excels his mother at her mighty art;
Offering to every weary traveller
His orient liquor in a crystal glass,
To quench the drouth of Phœbus; which as they taste
(For most do taste through fond intemperate thirst),
Soon as the potion works, their human countenance,
The express resemblance of the gods, is changed
Into some brutish form of wolf, or bear,
Or ounce, or tiger, hog, or bearded goat,
All other parts remaining as they were;
And they, so perfect in their misery,
Not once perceive their foul disfigurement,
But boast themselves more comely than before,
And all their friends and native home forget,
To roll with pleasure in a sensual sty.
Therefore, when any favoured of high Jove
Chances to pass through this adventurous glade,
Swift as the sparkle of a glancing star
I shoot from Heaven, to give him safe convoy,
As now I do. But first I must put off

COMUS

These my sky-robes spun out of Iris' woof,
And take the weeds and likeness of a swain
That to the service of this house belongs,
Who, with his soft pipe and smooth-dittied song,
Well knows to still the wild winds when they roar,
And hush the waving woods ; nor of less faith,
And in this office of his mountain watch
Likeliest, and nearest to the present aid
Of this occasion.   But I hear the tread
Of hateful steps ; I must be viewless now.

COMUS *enters, with a charming-rod in one hand, his
glass in the other ; with him a rout of monsters,
headed like sundry sorts of wild beasts, but otherwise
like men and women, their apparel glistering ; they
come in, making a riotous and unruly noise, with
torches in their hands.*

Comus. The star that bids the shepherd fold
Now the top of heaven doth hold ;
And the gilded car of day
His glowing axle doth allay
In the steep Atlantic stream ;
And the slope sun his upward beam
Shoots against the dusky pole ;
Pacing toward the other goal
Of his chamber in the east.
Meanwhile welcome joy and feast,
Midnight shout and revelry,
Tipsy dance and jollity.
Braid your locks with rosy twine,
Dropping odours, dropping wine.
Rigour now is gone to bed,
And Advice with scrupulous head,
Strict Age, and sour Severity,
With their grave saws, in slumber lie.
We, that are of purer fire,

THE STAR THAT BIDS THE SHEPHERD FOLD
NOW THE TOP OF HEAVEN DOTH HOLD

COMUS

Imitate the starry quire,
Who, in their nightly watchful spheres,
Lead in swift round the months and years.
The sounds and seas, with all their finny drove,
Now to the moon in wavering morrice move ;
And on the tawny sands and shelves
Trip the pert fairies and the dapper elves.
By dimpled brook and fountain brim,
The wood-nymphs, decked with daisies trim,
Their merry wakes and pastimes keep.
What hath night to do with sleep?
Night hath better sweets to prove,
Venus now wakes, and wakens Love.
Come, let us our rites begin,
'Tis only daylight that makes sin,
Which these dun shades will ne'er report.
Hail, Goddess of nocturnal sport,
Dark-veiled Cotytto, to whom the secret flame
Of midnight torches burns ; mysterious dame
That ne'er art called, but when the dragon womb
Of Stygian darkness spets her thickest gloom,
And makes one blot of all the air !
Stay thy cloudy ebon chair,
Wherein thou ridest with Hecat', and befriend
Us thy vowed priests, till utmost end
Of all thy due be done, and none left out ;
Ere the blabbing eastern scout,
The nice Morn on the Indian steep,
From her cabined loophole peep,
And to the tell-tale sun descry
Our concealed solemnity.
Come, knit hands, and beat the ground,
In a light fantastic round.   [*The Measure.*
  Break off, break off! I feel the different pace
Of some chaste footing near about this ground.
Run to your shrouds, within these brakes and trees ;
Our number may affright.   Some virgin sure

COMUS

(For so I can distinguish by mine art)
Benighted in these woods.   Now to my charms,
And to my wily trains ; I shall ere long
Be well stocked with as fair a herd as grazed
About my mother Circe.   Thus I hurl
My dazzling spells into the spongy air,
Of power to cheat the eye with blear illusion,
And give it false presentments, lest the place
And my quaint habits breed astonishment,
And put the damsel to suspicious flight ;
Which must not be, for that's against my course.
I, under fair pretence of friendly ends,
And well-placed words of glozing courtesy,
Baited with reasons not unplausible,
Wind me into the easy-hearted man,
And hug him into snares.   When once her eye
Hath met the virtue of this magic dust,
I shall appear some harmless villager,
Whom thrift keeps up about his country gear.
But here she comes ; I fairly step aside,
And hearken, if I may her business hear.

The LADY *enters.*

Lady. This way the noise was, if mine ear be true,
My best guide now.   Methought it was the sound
Of riot and ill-managed merriment,
Such as the jocund flute or gamesome pipe
Stirs up among the loose unlettered hinds,
When, for their teeming flocks and granges full,
In wanton dance they praise the bounteous Pan,
And thank the gods amiss.   I should be loth
To meet the rudeness and swilled insolence
Of such late wassailers ; yet, oh, where else
Shall I inform my unacquainted feet
In the blind mazes of this tangled wood ?
My brothers, when they saw me wearied out
With this long way, resolving here to lodge

COMUS

Under the spreading favour of these pines,
Stepped, as they said, to the next thicket side
To bring me berries, or such cooling fruit
As the kind hospitable woods provide.
They left me then, when the gray-hooded Even,
Like a sad votarist in palmer's weed,
Rose from the hindmost wheels of Phœbus' wain.
But where they are, and why they came not back,
Is now the labour of my thoughts.   'Tis likeliest
They had engaged their wandering steps too far,
And envious darkness, ere they could return,
Had stole them from me ; else, O thievish Night,
Why shouldst thou, but for some felonious end,
In thy dark lantern thus close up the stars,
That Nature hung in heaven, and filled their lamps
With everlasting oil, to give due light
To the misled and lonely traveller?
This is the place, as well as I may guess,
Whence even now the tumult of loud mirth
Was rife, and perfect in my listening ear,
Yet nought but single darkness do I find.
What might this be?   A thousand fantasies
Begin to throng into my memory,
Of calling shapes, and beckoning shadows dire,
And airy tongues that syllable men's names
On sands and shores and desert wildernesses.
These thoughts may startle well, but not astound
The virtuous mind, that ever walks attended
By a strong siding champion, Conscience.
Oh, welcome pure-eyed Faith, white-handed Hope,
Thou hovering angel girt with golden wings,
And thou unblemished form of Chastity !
I see ye visibly, and now believe
That he, the Supreme Good, to whom all things ill
Are but as slavish officers of vengeance,
Would send a glistering guardian, if need were,
To keep my life and honour unassailed.

COMUS

Was I deceived, or did a sable cloud
Turn forth her silver lining on the night?
I did not err, there does a sable cloud
Turn forth her silver lining on the night,
And casts a gleam over this tufted grove.
I cannot holloa to my brothers, but
Such noise as I can make to be heard farthest
I'll venture; for my new-enlivened spirits
Prompt me, and they perhaps are not far off.

Song

Sweet Echo, sweetest Nymph, that liv'st unseen
    Within thy airy shell
  By slow Meander's margent green,
And in the violet-embroidered vale,
    Where the love-lorn nightingale
Nightly to thee her sad song mourneth well;
Canst thou not tell me of a gentle pair
    That likest thy Narcissus are?
    Oh, if thou have
  Hid them in some flowery cave,
    Tell me but where,
Sweet Queen of Parley, Daughter of the Sphere!
So mayst thou be translated to the skies,
And give resounding grace to all Heaven's harmonies.

Comus. Can any mortal mixture of earth's mould
Breathe such divine enchanting ravishment?
Sure something holy lodges in that breast,
And with these raptures moves the vocal air
To testify his hidden residence.
How sweetly did they float upon the wings
Of Silence, through the empty-vaulted night,
At every fall smoothing the raven down
Of Darkness till it smiled. I have oft heard
My mother Circe with the Sirens three,
Amidst the flowery-kirtled Naiades

SWEET ECHO, SWEETEST NYMPH

COMUS

Culling their potent herbs, and baleful drugs ;
Who as they sung would take the prisoned soul
And lap it in Elysium ; Scylla wept,
And chid her barking waves into attention ;
And fell Charybdis murmured soft applause.
Yet they in pleasing slumber lulled the sense,
And in sweet madness robbed it of itself ;
But such a sacred and home-felt delight,
Such sober certainty of waking bliss,
I never heard till now.   I'll speak to her,
And she shall be my queen.   Hail, foreign wonder !
Whom, certain, these rough shades did never breed,
Unless the goddess that in rural shrine
Dwell'st here with Pan, or Silvan, by blest song
Forbidding every bleak unkindly fog
To touch the prosperous growth of this tall wood.
   Lady. Nay, gentle shepherd, ill is lost that praise
That is addressed to unattending ears ;
Not any boast of skill, but extreme shift
How to regain my severed company,
Compelled me to awake the courteous Echo
To give me answer from her mossy couch.
   Comus. What chance, good Lady, hath bereft you thus?
   Lady. Dim darkness, and this leafy labyrinth.
   Comus. Could that divide you from near-ushering guides?
   Lady. They left me weary on a grassy turf.
   Comus. By falsehood, or discourtesy, or why?
   Lady. To seek i' the valley some cool friendly spring.
   Comus. And left your fair side all unguarded, Lady?
   Lady. They were but twain, and purposed quick return.
   Comus. Perhaps forestalling night prevented them.
   Lady. How easy my misfortune is to hit !
   Comus. Imports their loss, beside the present need?
   Lady. No less than if I should my brothers lose.
   Comus. Were they of manly prime, or youthful bloom?
   Lady. As smooth as Hebe's their unrazored lips.
   Comus. Two such I saw, what time the laboured ox

COMUS

In his loose-traces from the furrow came,
And the swinked hedger at his supper sat.
I saw them under a green mantling vine
That crawls along the side of yon small hill,
Plucking ripe clusters from the tender shoots.
Their port was more than human, as they stood ;
I took it for a faery vision
Of some gay creatures of the element,
That in the colours of the rainbow live,
And play in the plighted clouds.   I was awestruck,
And as I passed, I worshipped.   If those you seek
It were a journey like the path to Heaven,
To help you find them.
    Lady.   Gentle villager,
What readiest way would bring me to that place ?
    Comus. Due west it rises from this shrubby point.
    Lady. To find out that, good shepherd, I suppose,
In such a scant allowance of starlight,
Would overtask the best land-pilot's art,
Without the sure guess of well-practised feet.
    Comus. I know each lane, and every alley green,
Dingle, or bushy dell of this wild wood,
And every bosky bourn from side to side,
My daily walks and ancient neighbourhood ;
And, if your stray attendance be yet lodged,
Or shroud within these limits, I shall know
Ere morrow wake, or the low-roosted lark
From her thatched pallet rouse ; if otherwise,
I can conduct you, Lady, to a low
But loyal cottage, where you may be safe
Till further quest.
    Lady.   Shepherd, I take thy word,
And trust thy honest-offered courtesy,
Which oft is sooner found in lowly sheds
With smoky rafters, than in tapestry halls
And courts of princes, where it first was named,
And yet is most pretended.   In a place

COMUS

Less warranted than this, or less secure,
I cannot be, that I should fear to change it.
Eye me, blest Providence, and square my trial
To my proportioned strength.   Shepherd, lead on.
                              [*Exeunt.*

99

COMUS

Enter the TWO BROTHERS.

Elder Brother. Unmuffle, ye faint stars; and thou, fair moon,
That wont'st to love the traveller's benison,
Stoop thy pale visage through an amber cloud,
And disinherit Chaos, that reigns here
In double night of darkness, and of shades;
Or if your influence be quite dammed up
With black usurping mists, some gentle taper,
Though a rush-candle from the wicker hole
Of some clay habitation, visit us
With thy long levelled rule of streaming light,
And thou shalt be our star of Arcady,
Or Tyrian Cynosure.
    Second Brother.   Or, if our eyes
Be barred that happiness, might we but hear
The folded flocks penned in their wattled cotes,
Or sound of pastoral reed with oaten stops,
Or whistle from the lodge, or village cock
Count the night watches to his feathery dames,
'Twould be some solace yet, some little cheering
In this close dungeon of innumerous boughs.
But, oh, that hapless virgin, our lost sister,
Where may she wander now, whither betake her
From the chill dew, amongst rude burs and thistles?
Perhaps some cold bank is her bolster now,
Or 'gainst the rugged bark of some broad elm
Leans her unpillowed head, fraught with sad fears.
What if in wild amazement and affright,
Or, while we speak, within the direful grasp
Of savage hunger, or of savage heat?
    Eld. Br. Peace, brother; be not over-exquisite
To cast the fashion of uncertain evils;
For, grant they be so, while they rest unknown,
What need a man forestall his date of grief,
And run to meet what he would most avoid?
Or, if they be but false alarms of fear,

COMUS

How bitter is such self-delusion!
I do not think my sister so to seek,
Or so unprincipled in virtue's book,
And the sweet peace that goodness bosoms ever,
As that the single want of light and noise
(Not being in danger, as I trust she is not),
Could stir the constant mood of her calm thoughts,
And put them into misbecoming plight.
Virtue could see to do what Virtue would
By her own radiant light, though sun and moon
Were in the flat sea sunk. And Wisdom's self
Oft seeks to sweet retired solitude,
Where, with her best nurse Contemplation,
She plumes her feathers, and lets grow her wings,
That, in the various bustle of resort,
Were all to-ruffled and sometimes impaired.
He that has light within his own clear breast
May sit i' the centre, and enjoy bright day;
But he that hides a dark soul and foul thoughts
Benighted walks under the mid-day sun;
Himself is his own dungeon.
 Sec. Br.   'Tis most true
That musing Meditation most affects
The pensive secrecy of desert cell,
Far from the cheerful haunt of men and herds,
And sits as safe as in a senate-house;
For who would rob a hermit of his weeds,
His few books, or his beads, or maple dish,
Or do his gray hairs any violence?
But Beauty, like the fair Hesperian tree
Laden with blooming gold, had need the guard
Of dragon-watch with unenchanted eye
To save her blossoms, and defend her fruit,
From the rash hand of bold Incontinence.
You may as well spread out the unsunned heaps
Of misers' treasure by an outlaw's den,
And tell me it is safe, and bid me hope

COMUS

Danger will wink on Opportunity,
And let a single helpless maiden pass
Uninjured in this wild surrounding waste.
Of night or loneliness it recks me not ;
I fear the dread events that dog them both,
Lest some ill-greeting touch attempt the person
Of our unowned sister.
    Eld. Br.   I do not, brother,
Infer as if I thought my sister's state
Secure without all doubt of controversy.
Yet where an equal poise of hope and fear
Does arbitrate the event, my nature is
That I incline to hope rather than fear,
And gladly banish squint suspicion.
My sister is not so defenceless left
As you imagine ; she has a hidden strength
Which you remember not.
    Sec. Br.   What hidden strength ?
Unless the strength of Heaven, if you mean that.
    Eld. Br. I mean that too, but yet a hidden strength,
Which, if Heaven gave it, may be termed her own.
'Tis chastity, my brother, chastity ;
She that has that is clad in complete steel,
And like a quivered nymph with arrows keen
May trace huge forests and unharboured heaths,
Infamous hills and sandy perilous wilds ;
Where, through the sacred rays of chastity,
No savage fierce, bandit or mountaineer
Will dare to soil her virgin purity.
Yea, there where very desolation dwells,
By grots and caverns shagged with horrid shades,
She may pass on with unblenched majesty,
Be it not done in pride, or in presumption.
Some say, no evil thing that walks by night,
In fog or fire, by lake or moorish fen,
Blue meagre hag, or stubborn unlaid ghost
That breaks his magic chains at curfew time,

COMUS

No goblin, or swart faery of the mine,
Hath hurtful power o'er true virginity.
Do you believe me yet, or shall I call
Antiquity from the old schools of Greece
To testify the arms of chastity?
Hence had the huntress Dian her dread bow,
Fair silver-shafted queen for ever chaste,
Wherewith she tamed the brinded lioness
And spotted mountain pard, but set at nought
The frivolous bolt of Cupid; gods and men
Feared her stern frown, and she was queen o' the woods.
What was that snaky-headed Gorgon shield
That wise Minerva wore, unconquered virgin,
Wherewith she freezed her foes to congealed stone,
But rigid looks of chaste austerity,
And noble grace that dashed brute violence
With sudden adoration and blank awe?
So dear to Heaven is saintly chastity,
That, when a soul is found sincerely so,
A thousand liveried angels lackey her,
Driving far off each thing of sin and guilt,
And in clear dream, and solemn vision,
Tell her of things that no gross ear can hear,
Till oft converse with heavenly habitants
Begin to cast a beam on the outward shape,
The unpolluted temple of the mind,
And turns it by degrees to the soul's essence,
Till all be made immortal.   But, when lust
By unchaste looks, loose gestures, and foul talk,
But most by lewd and lavish act of sin,
Lets in defilement to the inward parts,
The soul grows clotted by contagion
Imbodies, and imbrutes, till she quite lose
The divine property of her first being.
Such are those thick and gloomy shadows damp
Oft seen in charnel vaults and sepulchres,
Lingering and sitting by a new-made grave,

COMUS

As loth to leave the body that it loved,
And linked itself by carnal sensualty
To a degenerate and degraded state.

  Sec. Br. How charming is divine philosophy!
Not harsh and crabbed, as dull fools suppose,
But musical as is Apollo's lute,
And a perpetual feast of nectared sweets,
Where no crude surfeit reigns.

  Eld. Br.   List! list! I hear
Some far-off halloa break the silent air.

  Sec. Br. Methought so too; what should it be?

  Eld. Br.   For certain,
Either some one like us night-foundered here,
Or else some neighbour woodman, or, at worst,
Some roving robber calling to his fellows.

  Sec. Br. Heaven keep my sister! Again, again, and near
Best draw, and stand upon our guard.

  Eld. Br.   I'll halloa.
If he be friendly, he comes well; if not,
Defence is a good cause, and Heaven be for us!

The ATTENDANT SPIRIT *halloas and enters, habited
like a shepherd.*

That halloa I should know. What are you? speak.
Come not too near, you fall on iron stakes else.

  Spirit. What voice is that? my young lord, speak again.

  Sec. Br. O brother, 'tis my father's shepherd, sure.

  Eld.Br. Thyrsis! Whose artful strains have oft delayed
The huddling brook to hear his madrigal,
And sweetened every musk-rose of the dale.
How camest thou here, good swain? Hath any ram
Slipped from the fold, or young kid lost his dam,
Or straggling wether the pent flock forsook?
How could'st thou find this dark sequestered nook?

  Spirit. O my loved master's heir, and his next joy,
I came not here on such a trivial toy
As a strayed ewe, or to pursue the stealth

COMUS

Of pilfering wolf; not all the fleecy wealth
That doth enrich these downs is worth a thought
To this my errand, and the care it brought.
But oh, my virgin Lady, where is she?
How chance she is not in your company?

   Eld. Br. To tell thee sadly, Shepherd, without blame,
Or our neglect, we lost her as we came.

     Spirit. Ay me unhappy! then my fears are true.

     Eld. Br. What fears, good Thyrsis? Prithee briefly shew.

     Spirit. I'll tell ye; 'tis not vain or fabulous,
(Though so esteemed by shallow ignorance)
What the sage poets, taught by the heavenly Muse,
Storied of old in high immortal verse
Of dire Chimeras and enchanted isles,
And rifted rocks whose entrance leads to hell;
For such there be, but unbelief is blind.
Within the navel of this hideous wood,
Immured in cypress shades, a sorcerer dwells,
Of Bacchus and of Circe born, great Comus,
Deep skilled in all his mother's witcheries;
And here to every thirsty wanderer,
By sly enticement gives his baneful cup,
With many murmurs mixed, whose pleasing poison
The visage quite transforms of him that drinks,
And the inglorious likeness of a beast
Fixes instead, unmoulding reason's mintage
Charactered in the face. This have I learnt
Tending my flocks by i' the hilly crofts
That brow this bottom glade; whence night by night
He and his monstrous rout are heard to howl
Like stabled wolves, or tigers at their prey,
Doing abhorred rites to Hecate
In their obscured haunts of inmost bowers.
Yet have they many baits, and guileful spells
To inveigle and invite the unwary sense
Of them that pass unweeting by the way.
This evening late, by then the chewing flocks

Had ta'en their supper on the savoury herb
Of knot-grass dew-besprent, and were in fold,
I sat me down to watch upon a bank
With ivy canopied, and interwove
With flaunting honeysuckle, and began,
Wrapt in a pleasing fit of melancholy,
To meditate my rural minstrelsy,
Till fancy had her fill ; but ere a close
106

COMUS

The wonted roar was up amidst the woods,
And filled the air with barbarous dissonance ;
At which I ceased, and listened them a while,
Till an unusual stop of sudden silence
Gave respite to the drowsy frighted steeds
That draw the litter of close-curtained Sleep.
At last a soft and solemn-breathing sound
Rose like a steam of rich distilled perfumes,
And stole upon the air, that even Silence
Was took ere she was ware, and wished she might
Deny her nature, and be never more,
Still to be so displaced.   I was all ear,
And took in strains that might create a soul
Under the ribs of Death.   But, oh, ere long
Too well did I perceive it was the voice
Of my most honoured Lady, your dear sister.
Amazed I stood, harrowed with grief and fear ;
And 'O, poor hapless nightingale,' thought I,
'How sweet thou sing'st, how near the deadly snare !'
Then down the lawns I ran with headlong haste,
Through paths and turnings often trod by day,
Till guided by mine ear, I found the place
Where that damned wizard, hid in sly disguise
(For so by certain signs I knew) had met
Already, ere my best speed could prevent,
The aidless innocent lady, his wished prey ;
Who gently asked if he had seen such two,
Supposing him some neighbour villager.
Longer I durst not stay, but soon I guessed
Ye were the two she meant ; with that I sprung
Into swift flight, till I had found you here,
But further know I not.
    Sec. Br.   O night and shades,
How are ye joined with hell in triple knot
Against the unarmed weakness of one virgin,
Alone and helpless ! Is this the confidence
You gave me, brother ?

COMUS

Eld. Br.   Yes, and keep it still ;
Lean on it safely, not a period
Shall be unsaid for me.   Against the threats
Of malice or of sorcery, or that power
Which erring men call Chance, this I hold firm,—
Virtue may be assailed, but never hurt,
Surprised by unjust force, but not enthralled ;
Yea, even that which Mischief meant most harm
Shall in the happy trial prove most glory.
But evil on itself shall back recoil,
And mix no more with goodness, when at last
Gathered like scum, and settled to itself,
It shall be in eternal restless change
Self-fed and self-consumed.   If this fail,
The pillared firmament is rottenness,
And earth's base built on stubble.   But come, let's on !
Against the opposing will and arm of Heaven
May never this just sword be lifted up ;
But for that damned magician, let him be girt
With all the grisly legions that troop
Under the sooty flag of Acheron,
Harpies and hydras, or all the monstrous forms
'Twixt Africa and Ind, I'll find him out,
And force him to return his purchase back,
Or drag him by the curls to a foul death,
Cursed as his life.
     Spirit.   Alas ! good venturous youth,
I love thy courage yet, and bold emprise ;
But here thy sword can do thee little stead ;
Far other arms and other weapons must
Be those that quell the might of hellish charms ;
He with his bare wand can unthread thy joints,
And crumble all thy sinews.
     Eld. Br.   Why prithee, shepherd
How durst thou then thyself approach so near
As to make this relation ?
     Spirit.   Care and utmost shifts

COMUS

How to secure the Lady from surprisal
Brought to my mind a certain shepherd lad
Of small regard to see to, yet well skilled
In every virtuous plant and healing herb
That spreads her verdant leaf to the morning ray.
He loved me well, and oft would beg me sing,
Which when I did, he on the tender grass
Would sit, and hearken even to ecstasy ;
And in requital ope his leathern scrip,
And show me simples of a thousand names,
Telling their strange and vigorous faculties.
Amongst the rest a small unsightly root,
But of divine effect, he culled me out ;
The leaf was dark, and had prickles on it,
But in another country, as he said,
Bore a bright golden flower, but not in this soil ;
Unknown, and like esteemed, and the dull swain
Treads on it daily with his clouted shoon ;
And yet more med'cinal is it than that moly
That Hermes once to wise Ulysses gave ;
He called it hæmony, and gave it me,
And bade me keep it as of sovran use
'Gainst all enchantments, mildew blast, or damp,
Or ghastly Furies' apparition ;
I pursed it up, but little reckoning made,
Till now that this extremity compelled.
But now I find it true ; for by this means
I knew the foul enchanter, though disguised,
Entered the very lime-twigs of his spells,
And yet came off.   If you have this about you
(As I will give you when we go), you may
Boldly assault the necromancer's hall ;
Where if he be, with dauntless hardihood
And brandished blade rush on him, break his glass,
And shed the luscious liquor on the ground,
But seize his wand ; though he and his cursed crew
Fierce sign of battle make, and menace high,

COMUS

Or like the sons of Vulcan vomit smoke,
Yet will they soon retire, if he but shrink.
  Eld. Br. Thyrsis, lead on apace, I'll follow thee;
And some good Angel bear a shield before us!

*The Scene changes to a stately palace, set out with all
    manner of deliciousness; soft music, tables spread
    with all dainties.* COMUS *appears with his rabble,
    and the* LADY *set in an enchanted chair, to whom he
    offers his glass, which she puts by, and goes about to
    rise.*

  Comus. Nay, Lady, sit; if I but wave this wand,
Your nerves are all chained up in alabaster,
And you a statue; or as Daphne was,
Rootbound, that fled Apollo.
  Lady.   Fool, do not boast;
Thou canst not touch the freedom of my mind
With all thy charms, although this corporal rind
Thou hast immanacled, while Heaven sees good.
  Comus. Why are you vexed, Lady? Why do you frown?
Here dwell no frowns, nor anger; from these gates
Sorrow flies far.   See, here be all the pleasures
That fancy can beget on youthful thoughts,
When the fresh blood grows lively, and returns
Brisk as the April buds in primrose-season.
And first behold this cordial julep here,
That flames and dances in his crystal bounds,
With spirits of balm and fragrant syrups mixed.
Not that nepenthes, which the wife of Thone
In Egypt gave to Jove-born Helena,
Is of such power to stir up joy as this,
To life so friendly, or so cool to thirst.
Why should you be so cruel to yourself,
And to those dainty limbs which Nature lent
For gentle usage, and soft delicacy?
But you invert the covenants of her trust,
And harshly deal like an ill borrower

NAY, LADY, SIT; IF I BUT WAVE THIS WAND,
YOUR NERVES ARE ALL CHAINED UP IN ALABASTER

With that which you received on other terms,
Scorning the unexempt condition
By which all mortal frailty must subsist,
Refreshment after toil, ease after pain,
That have been tired all day without repast,
And timely rest have wanted ; but, fair virgin,
This will restore all soon.

    Lady.   'Twill not, false traitor !
'Twill not restore the truth and honesty
That thou hast banished from thy tongue with lies.
Was this the cottage and the safe abode
Thou told'st me of ? What grim aspects are these,
These ugly-headed monsters ? Mercy guard me !
Hence with thy brewed enchantments, foul deceiver !
Hast thou betrayed my credulous innocence
With vizored falsehood and base forgery,
And wouldst thou seek again to trap me here
With liquorish baits, fit to ensnare a brute ?
Were it a draught for Juno when she banquets,
I would not taste thy treasonous offer.   None
But such as are good men can give good things,
And that which is not good is not delicious
To a well-governed and wise appetite.

    Comus. O foolishness of men ! that lend their ears
To those budge doctors of the Stoic fur,
And fetch their precepts from the Cynic tub,
Praising the lean and sallow Abstinence.
Wherefore did Nature pour her bounties forth
With such a full and unwithdrawing hand,
Covering the earth with odours, fruits and flocks,
Thronging the seas with spawn innumerable,
But all to please, and sate the curious taste ?
And set to work millions of spinning worms,
That in their green shops weave the smooth-haired silk
To deck her sons, and, that no corner might
Be vacant of her plenty, in her own loins
She hutched the all-worshipped ore, and precious gems

COMUS

To store her children with.   If all the world
Should in a pet of temperance feed on pulse,
Drink the clear stream, and nothing wear but frieze,
The All-giver would be unthanked, would be unpraised,
Not half his riches known, and yet despised ;
And we would serve him as a grudging master,
As a penurious niggard of his wealth,
And live like Nature's bastards, not her sons,
Who would be quite surcharged with her own weight,
And strangled with her waste fertility ;
The earth cumbered, and the winged air darked with plumes ;
The herds would overmultitude their lords,
The sea o'erfraught would swell, and the unsought diamonds
Would so emblaze the forehead of the deep,
And so bestud with stars, that they below
Would grow inured to light, and come at last
To gaze upon the sun with shameless brows.
List, Lady, be not coy, and be not cozened
With that same vaunted name, Virginity.
Beauty is Nature's coin, must not be hoarded,
But must be current ; and the good thereof
Consists in mutual and partaken bliss,
Unsavoury in the enjoyment of itself ;
If you let slip time, like a neglected rose
It withers on the stalk with languished head.
Beauty is Nature's brag, and must be shown
In courts, at feasts, and high solemnities,
Where most may wonder at the workmanship.
It is for homely features to keep home,
They had their name thence ; coarse complexions
And cheeks of sorry grain will serve to ply
The sampler, and to tease the housewife's wool.
What need a vermeil-tinctured lip for that,
Love-darting eyes, or tresses like the morn ?
There was another meaning in these gifts ;
Think what, and be advised ; you are but young yet.
    Lady. I had not thought to have unlocked my lips

COMUS

In this unhallowed air, but that this juggler
Would think to charm my judgment, as mine eyes,
Obtruding false rules pranked in reason's garb.
I hate when Vice can bolt her arguments,
And Virtue has no tongue to check her pride.
Impostor, do not charge most innocent Nature,
As if she would her children should be riotous
With her abundance ; she, good cateress,
Means her provision only to the good,
That live according to her sober laws
And holy dictate of spare Temperance.
If every just man that now pines with want
Had but a moderate and beseeming share
Of that which lewdly-pampered Luxury
Now heaps upon some few with vast excess,
Nature's full blessings would be well dispensed
In unsuperfluous even proportion,
And she no whit encumbered with her store ;
And then the Giver would be better thanked,
His praise due paid ; for swinish Gluttony
Ne'er looks to Heaven amidst his gorgeous feast,
But with besotted base ingratitude
Crams, and blasphemes his Feeder.   Shall I go on?
Or have I said enough?   To him that dares
Arm his profane tongue with contemptuous words
Against the sun-clad power of Chastity,
Fain would I something say ;—yet to what end?
Thou hast nor ear, nor soul, to apprehend
The sublime notion, and high mystery
That must be uttered to unfold the sage
And serious doctrine of Virginity ;
And thou art worthy that thou shouldst not know
More happiness than this thy present lot.
Enjoy your dear wit, and gay rhetoric,
That hath so well been taught her dazzling fence ;
Thou art not fit to hear thyself convinced.
Yet, should I try, the uncontrolled worth

COMUS

Of this pure cause would kindle my rapt spirits
To such a flame of sacred vehemence,
That dumb things would be moved to sympathize,
And the brute Earth would lend her nerves, and shake,
Till all thy magic structures, reared so high,
Were shattered into heaps o'er thy false head.
   Comus. She fables not. I feel that I do fear
Her words set off by some superior power ;
And though not mortal, yet a cold shuddering dew
Dips me all o'er ; as when the wrath of Jove
Speaks thunder and the chains of Erebus
To some of Saturn's crew. I must dissemble,
And try her yet more strongly.—Come, no more !
This is mere moral babble, and direct
Against the canon laws of our foundation ;
I must not suffer this ; yet 'tis but the lees
And settlings of a melancholy blood.
But this will cure all straight ; one sip of this
Will bathe the drooping spirits in delight
Beyond the bliss of dreams. Be wise, and taste.

The BROTHERS *rush in with swords drawn, wrest his
glass out of his hand, and break it against the
ground ; his rout make sign of resistance, but are all
driven in. The* ATTENDANT SPIRIT *comes in.*

   Spirit. What ! have you let the false enchanter scape ?
O ye mistook ; ye should have snatched his wand
And bound him fast ; without his rod reversed,
And backward mutters of dissevering power,
We cannot free the lady, that sits here
In stony fetters fixed, and motionless ;
Yet stay, be not disturbed ; now I bethink me,
Some other means I have which may be used,
Which once of Meliboeus old I learnt,

COMUS

The soothest shepherd that e'er piped on plains.
  There is a gentle Nymph not far from hence,
That with moist curb sways the smooth Severn stream:
Sabrina is her name, a virgin pure;
Whilom she was the daughter of Locrine,
That had the sceptre from his father Brute.
She, guiltless damsel, flying the mad pursuit
Of her enraged stepdame, Guendolen,
Commended her fair innocence to the flood,
That stayed her flight with his cross-flowing course.
The water-nymphs, that in the bottom played,
Held up their pearled wrists and took her in,
Bearing her straight to aged Nereus' hall;
Who, piteous of her woes, reared her lank head,
And gave her to his daughters to imbathe
In nectared lavers strewed with asphodel,
And through the porch and inlet of each sense
Dropt in ambrosial oils, till she revived,
And underwent a quick immortal change,
Made Goddess of the river.   Still she retains
Her maiden gentleness, and oft at eve
Visits the herds along the twilight meadows,
Helping all urchin blasts, and ill-luck signs
That the shrewd meddling elf delights to make,
Which she with precious vialed liquors heals.
For which the shepherds at their festivals
Carol her goodness loud in rustic lays,
And throw sweet garland wreaths into her stream
Of pansies, pinks, and gaudy daffodils.
And, as the old swain said, she can unlock
The clasping charm, and thaw the numbing spell
If she be right invoked in warbled song;
For maidenhood she loves, and will be swift
To aid a virgin, such as was herself,
In hard-besetting need.   This will I try,
And add the power of some adjuring verse.

COMUS

Song

Sabrina fair,
   Listen where thou art sitting,
Under the glassy, cool, translucent wave,
   In twisted braids of lilies knitting
The loose train of thy amber-dropping hair;
   Listen for dear honour's sake,
   Goddess of the silver lake,
      Listen and save!

Listen and appear to us,
In name of great Oceanus,
By the earth-shaking Neptune's mace,
And Tethys' grave majestic pace;
By hoary Nereus' wrinkled look,
And the Carpathian wizard's hook;
By scaly Triton's winding shell,
And old soothsaying Glaucus' spell;
By Leucothea's lovely hands,
And her son that rules the strands;
By Thetis' tinsel-slippered feet,
And the songs of Sirens sweet;
By dead Parthenope's dear tomb,
And fair Ligea's golden comb,
Wherewith she sits on diamond rocks
Sleeking her soft alluring locks;
By all the nymphs that nightly dance
Upon thy streams with wily glance,
Rise, rise, and heave thy rosy head
From thy coral-paven bed,
And bridle in thy headlong wave,
Till thou our summons answered have.
      Listen and save!

SABRINA *rises, attended by Water-Nymphs, and sings*
   By the rushy-fringed bank,
   Where grows the willow and the osier dank,
     My sliding chariot stays;
   Thick set with agate, and the azurn sheen

SABRINA FAIR, LISTEN WHERE THOU ART SITTING,
UNDER THE GLASSY, COOL, TRANSLUCENT WAVE

COMUS

Of turkis blue, and emerald green,
   That in the channel strays ;
Whilst from off the waters fleet
Thus I set my printless feet
O'er the cowslip's velvet head,
   That bends not as I tread ;
Gentle swain, at thy request
   I am here.
   Spirit. Goddess dear,
We implore thy powerful hand
To undo the charmed band
Of true virgin here distressed
Through the force and through the wile
Of unblest enchanter vile.
   Sabrina. Shepherd, 'tis my office best
To help ensnared chastity.
Brightest Lady, look on me ;
Thus I sprinkle on thy breast
Drops that from my fountain pure,
I have kept of precious cure,
Thrice upon thy finger's tip,
Thrice upon thy rubied lip ;
Next this marble venomed seat
Smeared with gums of glutinous heat
I touch with chaste palms moist and cold.
Now the spell hath lost his hold ;
And I must haste ere morning hour
To wait in Amphitrite's bower.

SABRINA *descends, and the* LADY *rises out of her seat*

   Spirit. Virgin, daughter of Locrine,
Sprung of old Anchises' line,
May thy brimmed waves for this
Their full tribute never miss
From a thousand petty rills,
That tumble down the snowy hills ;
Summer drouth or singed air
Never scorch thy tresses fair,

COMUS

Nor wet October's torrent flood
Thy molten crystal fill with mud ;
May thy billows roll ashore
The beryl and the golden ore ;
May thy lofty head be crowned
With many a tower and terrace round,
And here and there thy banks upon
With groves of myrrh and cinnamon.
   Come, Lady, while Heaven lends us grace,
Let us fly this cursed place,
Lest the sorcerer us entice
With some other new device.
Not a waste or needless sound
Till we come to holier ground.
I shall be your faithful guide
Through this gloomy covert wide ;
And not many furlongs thence
Is your father's residence,
Where this night are met in state
Many a friend to gratulate
His wished presence, and beside
All the swains that there abide
With jigs and rural dance resort ;
We shall catch them at their sport,
And our sudden coming there
Will double all their mirth and cheer ;
Come, let us haste, the stars grow high,
But Night sits monarch yet in the mid sky.

*The Scene changes, presenting Ludlow town, and the
President's castle ; then come in country Dancers ;
after them the* ATTENDANT SPIRIT, *with the Two*
BROTHERS, *and the* LADY.

Song

   Spirit. Back, shepherds, back ! Enough your play,
Till next sunshine holiday.

COMUS

Here be, without duck or nod,
Other trippings to be trod
Of lighter toes, and such court guise
As Mercury did first devise
   With the mincing Dryades
On the lawns and on the leas.

*This second Song presents them to their Father and
Mother*

   Noble Lord, and Lady bright,
I have brought ye new delight ;
Here behold so goodly grown
Three fair branches of your own ;
Heaven hath timely tried their youth,
Their faith, their patience, and their truth ;
And sent them here through hard assays
With a crown of deathless praise,
To triumph in victorious dance
O'er sensual Folly and Intemperance.

The dances ended, the SPIRIT *epiloguizes*

   Spirit. To the ocean now I fly
And those happy climes that lie
Where day never shuts his eye,
Up in the broad fields of the sky ;
There I suck the liquid air
All amidst the gardens fair
Of Hesperus, and his daughters three
That sing about the golden tree.
Along the crisped shades and bowers
Revels the spruce and jocund Spring ;
The Graces, and the rosy-bosomed Hours,
Thither all their bounties bring ;
There eternal summer dwells ;
And west winds with musky wing
About the cedarn alleys fling
Nard and cassia's balmy smells.

123

COMUS

Iris there with humid bow
Waters the odorous banks, that blow
Flowers of more mingled hue
Than her purfled scarf can shew ;
And drenches with Elysian dew
(List, mortals, if your ears be true)
Beds of hyacinth and roses,
Where young Adonis oft reposes,
Waxing well of his deep wound
In slumber soft, and on the ground
Sadly sits the Assyrian queen.
But far above in spangled sheen
Celestial Cupid, her famed son, advanced
Holds his dear Psyche sweet entranced
After her wandering labours long,
Till free consent the gods among
Make her his eternal bride,
And from her fair unspotted side
Two blissful twins are to be born,
Youth and Joy ; so Jove hath sworn.

But now my task is smoothly done,
I can fly or I can run
Quickly to the green earth's end,
Where the bowed welkin slow doth bend ;
And from thence can soar as soon
To the corners of the moon.
Mortals that would follow me,
Love Virtue ; she alone is free ;
She can teach ye how to climb
Higher than the sphery chime ;
Or, if Virtue feeble were,
Heaven itself would stoop to her.

CELESTIAL CUPID, HER FAMED SON, ADVANCED
HOLDS HIS DEAR PSYCHE SWEET ENTRANCED

SAMSON AGONISTES

A DRAMATIC POEM

Arist. *Poet.* cap. 6—

Τραγῳδία μίμησις πράξεως σπωδαίας, etc.

Tragœdia est imitatio actionis seriæ, etc., per misericordiam et metum perficiens talium affectuum lustrationem.

THE PERSONS

SAMSON.

MANOAH, *the father of Samson.*	*Public Officer.*
DALILA, *his wife.*	*Messenger.*
HARAPHA, *of Gath.*	*Chorus of Danites.*

The Scene, before the Prison in Gaza.

THE ARGUMENT

Samson, made captive, blind, and now in the prison at Gaza, there to labour as in a common workhouse, on a festival day, in the general cessation from labour, comes forth into the open air, to a place nigh, somewhat retired, there to sit a while and bemoan his condition. Where he happens at length to be visited by certain friends and equals of his tribe, which make the Chorus, who seek to comfort him what they can; then by his old father Manoah, who endeavours the like and withal tells him his purpose to procure his liberty by ransom; lastly, that this feast was proclaimed by the Philistines as a day of thanksgiving for their deliverance from the hands of Samson, which yet more troubles him. Manoah then departs to prosecute his endeavour with the Philistine lords for Samson's redemption; who, in the meanwhile, is visited by other persons; and, lastly, by a public officer to require his coming to the feast before the lords and people, to play or show his strength in their presence. He at first refuses, dismissing the public officer with absolute denial to come; at length, persuaded inwardly that this was from God, he yields to go along with him, who came now the second time with great threatenings to fetch him. The Chorus yet remaining on the place, Manoah returns full of joyful hope, to procure ere long his son's deliverance; in the midst of which discourse an Hebrew comes in haste, confusedly at first, and afterwards more distinctly, relating the catastrophe, what Samson had done to the Philistines, and by accident to himself; wherewith the Tragedy ends.

SAMSON. *Attendant leading him.*

A LITTLE onward lend thy guiding hand
To these dark steps, a little further on;
For yonder bank hath choice of sun or shade;
There I am wont to sit, when any chance
Relieves me from my task of servile toil,
Daily in the common prison else enjoined me,
Where I, a prisoner chained, scarce freely draw
The air, imprisoned also, close and damp,
Unwholesome draught; but here I feel amends,
The breath of heaven fresh blowing, pure and sweet,

SAMSON AGONISTES

With day-spring born ; here leave me to respire.
This day a solemn feast the people hold
To Dagon, their sea-idol, and forbid
Laborious works ; unwillingly this rest
Their superstition yields me ; hence, with leave
Retiring from the popular noise, I seek
This unfrequented place to find some ease,
Ease to the body some, none to the mind
From restless thoughts, that, like a deadly swarm
Of hornets armed, no sooner found alone
But rush upon me thronging, and present
Times past, what once I was, and what am now.
Oh, wherefore was my birth from Heaven foretold
Twice by an Angel, who, at last, in sight
Of both my parents, all in flames ascended
From off the altar where an offering burned,
As in a fiery column charioting
His godlike presence, and from some great act
Or benefit revealed to Abraham's race ?
Why was my breeding ordered and prescribed
As of a person separate to God,
Designed for great exploits, if I must die
Betrayed, captived, and both my eyes put out,
Made of my enemies the scorn and gaze ;
To grind in brazen fetters under task
With this heaven-gifted strength ? O glorious strength,
Put to the labour of a beast, debased
Lower than bondslave ! Promise was, that I
Should Israel from the Philistian yoke deliver ;
Ask for this great deliverer now, and find him
Eyeless in Gaza, at the mill with slaves,
Himself in bonds under Philistian yoke.
Yet stay, let me not rashly call in doubt
Divine prediction ; what if all foretold
Had been fulfilled but through mine own default ?
Whom have I to complain of but myself ?
Who this high gift of strength committed to me,

SAMSON

SAMSON AGONISTES

In what part lodged, how easily bereft me,
Under the seal of silence could not keep,
But weakly to a woman must reveal it,
O'ercome with importunity and tears.
O impotence of mind in body strong!
But what is strength without a double share
Of wisdom? vast, unwieldy, burthensome,
Proudly secure, yet liable to fall
By weakest subtleties ; not made to rule,
But to subserve where wisdom bears command.
God, when he gave me strength, to show withal
How slight the gift was, hung it in my hair.
But peace! I must not quarrel with the will
Of highest dispensation, which herein
Haply had ends above my reach to know.
Suffices that to me strength is my bane,
And proves the source of all my miseries,
So many, and so huge, that each apart
Would ask a life to wail ; but, chief of all,
O loss of sight, of thee I most complain!
Blind among enemies, O worse than chains.
Dungeon, or beggary, or decrepit age!
Light, the prime work of God, to me is extinct,
And all her various objects of delight
Annulled, which might in part my grief have eased.
Inferior to the vilest now become
Of man or worm, the vilest here excel me ;
They creep, yet see ; I, dark in light, exposed
To daily fraud, contempt, abuse, and wrong,
Within doors, or without, still as a fool,
In power of others, never in my own ;
Scarce half I seem to live, dead more than half.
O dark, dark, dark, amid the blaze of noon,
Irrecoverably dark, total eclipse
Without all hope of day!
O first-created beam, and thou great Word,
" Let there be light, and light was over all,"

SAMSON AGONISTES

Why am I thus bereaved thy prime decree?
The sun to me is dark
And silent as the moon,
When she deserts the night,
Hid in her vacant interlunar cave.
Since light so necessary is to life,
And almost life itself, if it be true
That light is in the soul,
She all in every part, why was the sight
To such a tender ball as the eye confined,
So obvious and so easy to be quenched?
And not, as feeling, through all parts diffused,
That she might look at will through every pore?
Then had I not been thus exiled from light,
As in the land of darkness, yet in light,
To live a life half dead, a living death,
And buried ; but, O yet more miserable!
Myself my sepulchre, a moving grave,
Buried, yet not exempt,
By privilege of death and burial,
From worst of other evils, pains, and wrongs,
But made hereby obnoxious more
To all the miseries of life,
Life in captivity
Among inhuman foes.
But who are these? for with joint pace I hear
The tread of many feet steering this way ;
Perhaps my enemies, who come to stare
At my affliction, and perhaps to insult,
Their daily practice to afflict me more.
    Chorus. This, this is he, softly a while,
Let us not break in upon him.
O change beyond report, thought, or belief!
See how he lies at random, carelessly diffused,
With languished head unpropt,
As one past hope, abandoned,
And by himself given over ;

SAMSON AGONISTES

In slavish habit, ill-fitted weeds,
O'er-worn and soiled.
Or do my eyes misrepresent? Can this be he,
That heroic, that renowned,
Irresistible Samson? whom, unarmed
No strength of man, or fiercest wild beast, could withstand;
Who tore the lion as the lion tears the kid;
Ran on embattled armies clad in iron,
And, weaponless himself,
Made arms ridiculous, useless the forgery
Of brazen shield and spear, the hammered cuirass,
Chalybean-tempered steel, and frock of mail
Adamantean proof!
But safest he who stood aloof,
When insupportably his foot advanced,
In scorn of their proud arms and warlike tools,
Spurned them to death by troops. The bold Ascalonite
Fled from his lion ramp; old warriors turned
Their plated backs under his heel,
Or, grovelling, soiled their crested helmets in the dust.
Then with what trivial weapon came to hand,
The jaw of a dead ass, his sword of bone,
A thousand foreskins fell, the flower of Palestine,
In Ramath-lechi, famous to this day.
Then by main force pulled up, and on his shoulders bore,
The gates of Azza, post and massy bar,
Up to the hill by Hebron, seat of giants old—
No journey of a Sabbath-day, and loaded so—
Like whom the Gentiles feign to bear up heaven.
Which shall I first bewail,
Thy bondage or lost sight,
Prison within prison
Inseparably dark?
Thou art become (O worst imprisonment!)
The dungeon of thyself; thy soul,
(Which men enjoying sight oft without cause complain,)
Imprisoned now indeed,

SAMSON AGONISTES

In real darkness of the body dwells,
Shut up from outward light
To incorporate with gloomy night;
For inward light, alas!
Puts forth no visual beam.
O mirror of our fickle state,
Since man on earth, unparalleled,
The rarer thy example stands,
By how much from the top of wondrous glory,
Strongest of mortal men,
To lowest pitch of abject fortune thou art fallen.
For him I reckon not in high estate
Whom long descent of birth,
Or the sphere of fortune, raises;
But thee, whose strength, while virtue was her mate,
Might have subdued the earth,
Universally crowned with highest praises.

   Sams. I hear the sound of words; their sense the air
Dissolves, unjointed, ere it reach my ear.

   Cho. He speaks; let us draw nigh. Matchless in might,
The glory late of Israel, now the grief;
We come, thy friends and neighbours not unknown,
From Eshtaol and Zora's fruitful vale,
To visit or bewail thee; or, if better,
Counsel or consolation we may bring,
Salve to thy sores; apt words have power to swage
The tumours of a troubled mind,
And are as balm to festered wounds.

   Sams. Your coming, friends, revives me; for I learn
Now of my own experience, not by talk,
How counterfeit a coin they are who "friends"
Bear in their superscription (of the most
I would be understood); in prosperous days
They swarm, but in adverse withdraw their head,
Not to be found, though sought. Ye see, O friends,
How many evils have enclosed me round;
Yet that which was the worst now least afflicts me,

SAMSON AGONISTES

Blindness; for, had I sight, confused with shame,
How could I once look up, or heave the head,
Who, like a foolish pilot, have shipwracked
My vessel trusted to me from above,
Gloriously rigged, and for a word, a tear,
Fool! have divulged the secret gift of God
To a deceitful woman? Tell me, friends,
Am I not sung and proverbed for a fool
In every street? do they not say, "How well
Are come upon him his deserts"? Yet why?
Immeasurable strength they might behold
In me, of wisdom nothing more than mean;
This with the other should at least have paired;
These two, proportioned ill, drove me transverse.
  Cho. Tax not divine disposal; wisest men
Have erred, and by bad women been deceived;
And shall again, pretend they ne'er so wise.
Deject not, then, so overmuch thyself,
Who hast of sorrow thy full load besides.
Yet, truth to say, I oft have heard men wonder
Why thou shouldst wed Philistian women rather
Than of thine own tribe, fairer, or as fair,
At least of thy own nation, and as noble.
  Sams. The first I saw at Timna, and she pleased
Me, not my parents that I sought to wed
The daughter of an infidel; they knew not
That what I motioned was of God; I knew
From intimate impulse, and therefore urged
The marriage on, that, by occasion hence,
I might begin Israel's deliverance,
The work to which I was divinely called.
She, proving false, the next I took to wife
(Oh that I never had! fond wish too late!)
Was in the vale of Sorec, Dalila,
That specious monster, my accomplished snare.
I thought it lawful from my former act,
And the same end, still watching to oppress

Israel's oppressors ; of what now I suffer
She was not the prime cause, but I myself,
Who, vanquished with a peal of words, (O weakness!)
Gave up my fort of silence to a woman.
   Cho. In seeking just occasion to provoke
The Philistine, thy country's enemy,
Thou never wast amiss, I bear thee witness ;
Yet Israel still serves, with all his sons.
   Sams. That fault I take not on me, but transfer
On Israel's governors and heads of tribes,
Who, seeing those great acts which God had done
Singly by me against their conquerors,
Acknowledged not, or not at all considered,
Deliverance offered.   I, on the other side,
Used no ambition to commend my deeds ;
The deeds themselves, though mute, spoke loud the doer.
But they persisted deaf, and would not seem
To count them things worth notice, till at length,
Their lords, the Philistines, with gathered powers,
Entered Judea, seeking me who then
Safe to the rock of Etham was retired,
Not flying, but forecasting in what place
To set upon them, what advantaged best.
Meanwhile, the men of Judah, to prevent
The harass of their land, beset me round ;
I willingly on some conditions came
Into their hands, and they as gladly yield me
To the uncircumcised a welcome prey,
Bound with two cords.   But cords to me were threads
Touched with the flame ; on their whole host I flew
Unarmed, and with a trivial weapon felled
Their choicest youth ; they only lived who fled.
Had Judah that day joined, or one whole tribe,
They had by this possessed the towers of Gath,
And lorded over them whom now they serve.
But what more oft, in nations grown corrupt,
And by their vices brought to servitude,

DALILA

Than to love bondage more than liberty,
Bondage with ease than strenuous liberty,
And to despise, or envy, or suspect,
Whom God hath of His special favour raised
As their deliverer? If he aught begin,
How frequent to desert him, and at last
To heap ingratitude on worthiest deeds!

  Cho. Thy words to my remembrance bring
How Succoth and the fort of Penuel
Their great deliverer contemned,
The matchless Gideon, in pursuit
Of Madian, and her vanquished kings;
And how ingrateful Ephraim
Had dealt with Jephtha, who, by argument,
Not worse than by his shield and spear,
Defended Israel from the Ammonite,
Had not his prowess quelled their pride
In that sore battle, when so many died
Without reprieve, adjudged to death,
For want of well pronouncing *Shibboleth*.

  Sams. Of such examples add me to the roll;
Me easily, indeed, mine may neglect,
But God's proposed deliverance not so.

  Cho. Just are the ways of God,
And justifiable to men,
Unless there be who think not God at all;
If any be, they walk obscure;
For of such doctrine never was there school,
But the heart of the fool,
And no man therein doctor but himself.

  Yet more there be who doubt His ways not just,
As to His own edicts found contradicting,
Then give the reins to wandering thought,
Regardless of His glory's diminution;
Till, by their own perplexities involved,
They ravel more, still less resolved,
But never find self-satisfying solution.

SAMSON AGONISTES

As if they would confine the Interminable,
And tie Him to His own prescript,
Who made our laws to bind us, not Himself,
And hath full right to exempt
Whomso it pleases Him by choice
From national obstriction, without taint
Of sin, or legal debt;
For with His own laws He can best dispense.
He would not else, who never wanted means,
Nor in respect of the enemy just cause,
To set His people free,
Have prompted this heroic Nazarite,
Against his vow of strictest purity,
To seek in marriage that fallacious bride,
Unclean, unchaste.
    Down, reason, then; at least, vain reasonings down;
Though reason here aver
That moral verdict quits her of unclean;
Unchaste was subsequent; her stain, not his.
    But see, here comes thy reverend sire
With careful step, locks white as down,
Old Manoah; advise
Forthwith how thou oughtst to receive him.
    Sams. Ay me! another inward grief, awaked
With mention of that name, renews the assault.
    Manoah. Brethren, and men of Dan (for such ye seem,
Though in this uncouth place), if old respect,
As I suppose, towards your once gloried friend,
My son, now captive, hither hath informed
Your younger feet, while mine cast back with age
Came lagging after, say if he be here.
    Cho. As signal now in low dejected state,
As erst in highest, behold him where he lies.
    Man. O miserable change! is this the man,
That invincible Samson, far renowned,
The dread of Israel's foes, who, with a strength
Equivalent to angels', walked their streets,

142

MANOAH

SAMSON AGONISTES

None offering fight ; who, single combatant,
Duelled their armies ranked in proud array,
Himself an army, now unequal match
To save himself against a coward armed
At one spear's length ? O ever-failing trust
In mortal strength ! and, oh, what not in man
Deceivable and vain ! Nay, what thing good
Prayed for, but often proves our woe, our bane ?
I prayed for children, and thought barrenness
In wedlock a reproach ; I gained a son,
And such a son as all men hailed me happy ;
Who would be now a father in my stead ?
Oh, wherefore did God grant me my request,
And as a blessing with such pomp adorned ?
Why are His gifts desirable, to tempt
Our earnest prayers, then, given with solemn hand
As graces, draw a scorpion's tail behind ?
For this did the Angel twice descend ? for this
Ordained thy nurture holy, as of a plant
Select and sacred, glorious for awhile,
The miracle of men ; then in an hour
Ensnared, assaulted, overcome, led bound,
Thy foes' derision, captive, poor and blind,
Into a dungeon thrust, to work with slaves ?
Alas ! methinks whom God hath chosen once
To worthiest deeds, if he through frailty err,
He should not so o'erwhelm, and as a thrall
Subject him to so foul indignities,
Be it but for honour's sake of former deeds.
　　Sams. Appoint not heavenly disposition, father.
Nothing of all these evils hath befallen me
But justly ; I myself have brought them on,
Sole author I, sole cause.   If aught seem vile,
As vile hath been my folly, who have profaned
The mystery of God given me under pledge
Of vow, and have betrayed it to a woman,
A Canaanite, my faithless enemy.

SAMSON AGONISTES

This well I knew, nor was at all surprised,
But warned by oft experience ; did not she
Of Timna first betray me, and reveal
The secret wrested from me in her height
Of nuptial love professed, carrying it straight
To them who had corrupted her, my spies
And rivals?   In this other was there found
More faith, who, also in her prime of love,
Spousal embraces, vitiated with gold,
Though offered only, by the scent conceived
Her spurious first-born, treason against me?
Thrice she assayed, with flattering prayers and sighs,
And amorous reproaches, to win from me
My capital secret ; in what part my strength
Lay stored, in what part summed, that she might know ;
Thrice I deluded her, and turned to sport
Her importunity, each time perceiving
How openly and with what impudence
She purposed to betray me, and (which was worse
Than undissembled hate) with what contempt
She sought to make me traitor to myself.
Yet the fourth time, when, mustering all her wiles,
With blandished parleys, feminine assaults,
Tongue-batteries, she surceased not day nor night
To storm me, over-watched and wearied out,
At times when men seek most repose and rest,
I yielded, and unlocked her all my heart,
Who, with a grain of manhood well resolved,
Might easily have shook off all her snares ;
But foul effeminacy held me yoked
Her bondslave !   O indignity, O blot
To honour and religion ! servile mind
Rewarded well with servile punishment !
The base degree to which I now am fallen,
These rags, this grinding, is not yet so base
As was my former servitude, ignoble,
Unmanly, ignominious, infamous,

True slavery ; and that blindness worse than this,
That saw not how degenerately I served.

    Man. I cannot praise thy marriage choices, son,
Rather approved them not ; but thou didst plead
Divine impulsion prompting how thou mightst
Find some occasion to infest our foes.
I state not that ; this I am sure, our foes
Found soon occasion thereby to make thee
Their captive, and their triumph ; thou the sooner
Temptation found'st, or over-potent charms,
To violate the sacred trust of silence
Deposited within thee, which to have kept
Tacit was in thy power ; true ; and thou bear'st
Enough, and more, the burden of that fault ;
Bitterly hast thou paid, and still art paying,
That rigid score.   A worse thing yet remains ;
This day the Philistines a popular feast
Here celebrate in Gaza, and proclaim
Great pomp, and sacrifice, and praises loud,
To Dagon, as their god, who hath delivered
Thee, Samson, bound and blind, into their hands,
Them out of thine, who slew'st them many a slain.
So Dagon shall be magnified, and God,
Besides whom is no god, compared with idols,
Disglorified, blasphemed, and had in scorn
By the idolatrous rout amidst their wine ;
Which to have come to pass by means of thee,
Samson, of all thy sufferings think the heaviest,
Of all reproach the most with shame that ever
Could have befallen thee and thy father's house.

    Sams. Father, I do acknowledge and confess
That I this honour, I this pomp have brought
To Dagon, and advanced his praises high
Among the heathen round ; to God have brought
Dishonour, obloquy, and oped the mouths
Of idolists and atheists ; have brought scandal
To Israel, diffidence of God, and doubt

SAMSON AGONISTES

In feeble hearts, propense enough before
To waver, or fall off and join with idols;
Which is my chief affliction, shame and sorrow,
The anguish of my soul, that suffers not
Mine eye to harbour sleep, or thoughts to rest
This only hope relieves me, that the strife
With me hath end; all the contest is now
'Twixt God and Dagon; Dagon hath presumed,
Me overthrown, to enter lists with God,
His deity comparing and preferring
Before the God of Abraham.   He, be sure,
Will not connive, or linger, thus provoked,
But will arise, and His great name assert.
Dagon must stoop, and shall ere long receive
Such a discomfit, as shall quite despoil him
Of all these boasted trophies won on me,
And with confusion blank his worshippers.
   Man. With cause this hope relieves thee, and these words
I as a prophecy receive; for God,
Nothing more certain, will not long defer
To vindicate the glory of His name
Against all competition, nor will long
Endure it doubtful whether God be Lord,
Or Dagon.   But for thee what shall be done?
Thou must not in the meanwhile, here forgot,
Lie in this miserable loathsome plight,
Neglected.   I already have made way
To some Philistian lords, with whom to treat
About thy ransom; well they may by this
Have satisfied their utmost of revenge
By pains and slaveries, worse than death, inflicted
On thee, who now no more canst do them harm.
   Sams. Spare that proposal, father; spare the trouble
Of that solicitation; let me here,
As I deserve, pay on my punishment,
And expiate, if possible, my crime,
Shameful garrulity.   To have revealed

SAMSON AGONISTES

Secrets of *men*, the secrets of a friend,
How heinous had the fact been, how deserving
Contempt and scorn of all, to be excluded
All friendship, and avoided as a blab,
The mark of fool set on his front!
But I *God's* counsel have not kept; His holy secret
Presumptuously have published, impiously,
Weakly at least, and shamefully, a sin
That Gentiles in their parables condemn
To their abyss and horrid pains confined.

    Man. Be penitent, and for thy fault contrite;
But act not in thy own affliction, son.
Repent the sin; but, if the punishment
Thou canst avoid, self-preservation bids;
Or the execution leave to high disposal,
And let another hand, not thine, exact
Thy penal forfeit from thyself. Perhaps
God will relent, and quit thee all His debt;
Who ever more approves, and more accepts
(Best pleased with humble and filial submission)
Him who, imploring mercy, sues for life,
Than who, self-rigorous, chooses death as due;
Which argues over-just, and self-displeased
For self-offence, more than for God offended.
Reject not, then, what offered means who knows
But God hath set before us, to return thee
Home to thy country and His sacred house,
Where thou may'st bring thy offerings to avert
His further ire, with prayers and vows renewed.

    Sams. His pardon I implore; but as for life
To what end should I seek it? When in strength
All mortals I excelled, and great in hopes,
With youthful courage, and magnanimous thoughts
Of birth from Heaven foretold, and high exploits,
Full of divine instinct, after some proof
Of acts indeed heroic, far beyond
The sons of Anak, famous now and blazed,

149

SAMSON AGONISTES

Fearless of danger, like a petty god
I walked about, admired of all, and dreaded
On hostile ground, none daring my affront.
Then, swollen with pride, into the snare I fell
Of fair fallacious looks, venereal trains,
Softened with pleasure and voluptuous life,
At length to lay my head, and hallowed pledge
Of all my strength in the lascivious lap
Of a deceitful concubine, who shore me,
Like a tame wether, all my precious fleece,
Then turned me out ridiculous, despoiled,
Shaven, and disarmed among mine enemies.

  Cho. Desire of wine and all delicious drinks,
Which many a famous warrior overturns,
Thou couldst repress ; nor did the dancing ruby,
Sparkling out-poured, the flavour or the smell,
Or taste that cheers the heart of gods and men,
Allure thee from the cool crystalline stream.

  Sams. Wherever fountain or fresh current flowed
Against the eastern ray, translucent, pure
With touch ethereal of heaven's fiery rod,
I drank, from the clear milky juice allaying
Thirst, and refreshed ; nor envied them the grape
Whose heads that turbulent liquor fills with fumes.

  Cho. O madness, to think use of strongest wines
And strongest drinks our chief support of health,
When God, with these forbidden, made choice to rear
His mighty champion, strong above compare,
Whose drink was only from the liquid brook !

  Sams. But what availed this temperance, not complete
Against another object more enticing ?
What boots it at one gate to make defence,
And at another to let in the foe,
Effeminately vanquished ? by which means
Now blind, disheartened, shamed, dishonoured, quelled,
To what can I be useful ? wherein serve
My nation, and the work from Heaven imposed ?

SAMSON AGONISTES

But to sit idle on the household hearth,
A burdenous drone ; to visitants a gaze,
Or pitied object, these redundant locks,
Robustious to no purpose, clustering down,
Vain monument of strength ; till length of years
And sedentary numbness craze my limbs
To a contemptible old age obscure.
Here rather let me drudge, and earn my bread,
Till vermin, or the draff of servile food,
Consume me, and oft-invocated death
Hasten the welcome end of all my pains.
   Man. Wilt thou then serve the Philistines with that gift
Which was expressly given thee to annoy them ?
Better at home lie bed-rid, not only idle,
Inglorious, unemployed, with age outworn.
But God, who caused a fountain, at thy prayer,
From the dry ground to spring, thy thirst to allay
After the brunt of battle, can as easy
Cause light again within thy eyes to spring,
Wherewith to serve Him better than thou hast ;
And I persuade me so ; why else this strength
Miraculous yet remaining in those locks ?
His might continues in thee not for nought,
Nor shall his wondrous gifts be frustrate thus.
   Sams. All otherwise to me my thoughts portend,
That these dark orbs no more shall treat with light,
Nor the other light of life continue long,
But yield to double darkness nigh at hand ;
So much I feel my genial spirits droop,
My hopes all flat : Nature within me seems
In all her functions weary of herself ;
My race of glory run, and race of shame,
And I shall shortly be with them that rest.
   Man. Believe not these suggestions which proceed
From anguish of the mind, and humours black
That mingle with thy fancy.   I, however,
Must not omit a father's timely care

To prosecute the means of thy deliverance
By ransom, or how else ; meanwhile be calm,
And healing words from these thy friends admit. [*Exit.*
  Sams. Oh that torment should not be confined
To the body's wounds and sores,
With maladies innumerable,
In heart, head, breast, and reins,
But must secret passage find
To the inmost mind,
There exercise all his fierce accidents,
And on her purest spirits prey,
As on entrails, joints, and limbs,
With answerable pains, but more intense,
Though void of corporal sense !
  My griefs not only pain me,
As a lingering disease,
But, finding no redress, ferment and rage ;
Nor less than wounds immedicable
Rankle, and fester, and gangrene,
To black mortification.
Thoughts, my tormentors, armed with deadly stings,
Mangle my apprehensive tenderest parts,
Exasperate, exulcerate, and raise
Dire inflammation, which no cooling herb
Or medicinal liquor can assuage,
Nor breath of vernal air from snowy Alp.
Sleep hath forsook and given me o'er
To death's benumbing opium as my only cure ;
Thence faintings, swoonings of despair,
And sense of Heaven's desertion.
  I was His nursling once, and choice delight,
His destined from the womb,
Promised by heavenly message twice descending.
Under His special eye
Abstemious I grew up, and thrived amain ;
He led me on to mightiest deeds,
Above the nerve of mortal arm,

SAMSON AGONISTES

Against the uncircumcised, our enemies ;
But now hath cast me off as never known,
And to those cruel enemies,
Whom I, by His appointment, had provoked,
Left me all helpless, with the irreparable loss
Of sight, reserved alive to be repeated
The subject of their cruelty or scorn.
Nor am I in the list of them that hope ;
Hopeless are all my evils, all remediless.
This one prayer yet remains, might I be heard,
No long petition ; speedy death,
The close of all my miseries, and the balm.
   Chò. Many are the sayings of the wise,
In ancient and in modern books enrolled,
Extolling patience as the truest fortitude ;
And to the bearing well of all calamities,
All chances incident to man's frail life,
Consolatories writ
With studied argument, and much persuasion sought,
Lenient of grief and anxious thought ;
But with the afflicted, in his pangs, their sound
Little prevails, or rather seems a tune
Harsh, and of dissonant mood from his complaint,
Unless he feel within
Some source of consolation from above,
Secret refreshings, that repair his strength,
And fainting spirits uphold.
   God of our fathers ! what is man,
That thou, towards him, with hand so various,
(Or might I say contrarious ?)
Temper'st thy providence through his short course,
Not evenly, as thou rulest
The angelic orders, and inferior creatures mute,
Irrational and brute ?
Nor do I name of men the common rout,
That, wandering loose about,
Grow up and perish, as the summer fly,

SAMSON AGONISTES

Heads without name, no more remembered ;
But such as thou hast solemnly elected,
With gifts and graces eminently adorned,
To some great work, thy glory,
And people's safety, which in part they effect ;
Yet toward these, thus dignified, thou oft,
Amidst their height of noon,
Changest thy countenance and thy hand, with no regard
Of highest favours past
From thee on them, or them to thee of service.
    Nor only dost degrade them, or remit
To life obscured, which were a fair dismission,
But throw'st them lower than thou didst exalt them high ;
Unseemly falls in human eye,
Too grievous for the trespass or omission ;
Oft leavest them to the hostile sword
Of heathen and profane, their carcasses
To dogs and fowls a prey, or else captived,
Or to the unjust tribunals, under change of times,
And condemnation of the ingrateful multitude.
If these they scape, perhaps in poverty
With sickness and disease thou bow'st them down,
Painful diseases and deformed,
In crude old age ;
Though not disordinate, yet causeless suffering
The punishment of dissolute days ; in fine,
Just or unjust, alike seem miserable,
For oft alike both come to evil end.
    So deal not with this once thy glorious champion,
The image of thy strength, and mighty minister,
What do I beg ? how hast thou dealt already ?
Behold him in this state calamitous, and turn
His labours, for thou canst, to peaceful end.
    But who is this, what thing of sea or land ?
Female of sex it seems,
That, so bedecked, ornate, and gay,
Comes this way, sailing

SAMSON AGONISTES

Like a stately ship
Of Tarsus, bound for the isles
Of Javan or Gadire,
With all her bravery on, and tackle trim,
Sails filled, and streamers waving,
Courted by all the winds that hold them play,
An amber scent of odorous perfume
Her harbinger, a damsel train behind.
Some rich Philistian matron she may seem,
And now at nearer view, no other certain
Than Dalila thy wife.
   Sams. My wife! my traitress! let her not come near me.
   Cho. Yet on she moves, now stands and eyes thee, fixed,
About to have spoke; but now, with head declined,
Like a fair flower surcharged with dew, she weeps,
And words addressed seem into tears dissolved,
Wetting the borders of her silken veil:
But now again she makes address to speak.
   Dal. With doubtful feet and wavering resolution
I came, still dreading thy displeasure, Samson;
Which to have merited, without excuse,
I cannot but acknowledge; yet, if tears
May expiate (though the fact more evil drew
In the perverse event than I foresaw),
My penance hath not slackened, though my pardon
No way assured. But conjugal affection,
Prevailing over fear and timorous doubt,
Hath led me on, desirous to behold
Once more thy face, and know of thy estate,
If aught in my ability may serve
To lighten what thou sufferest, and appease
Thy mind with what amends is in my power,
Though late, yet in some part to recompense
My rash but more unfortunate misdeed.
   Sams. Out, out, hyæna! these are thy wonted arts,
And arts of every woman false like thee,
To break all faith, all vows, deceive, betray,

Then, as repentant, to submit, beseech,
And reconcilement move with feigned remorse,
Confess, and promise wonders in her change ;
Not truly penitent, but chief to try
Her husband, how far urged his patience bears,
His virtue or weakness which way to assail ;
Then with more cautious and instructed skill
Again transgresses, and again submits ;
That wisest and best men, full oft beguiled,
With goodness principled not to reject
The penitent, but ever to forgive,
Are drawn to wear out miserable days,
Entangled with a poisonous bosom snake,
If not by quick destruction soon cut off,
As I by thee, to ages an example.
    Dal. Yet hear me, Samson ; not that I endeavour
To lessen or extenuate my offence,
But that, on the other side, if it be weighed
By itself, with aggravations not surcharged,
Or else with just allowance counterpoised,
I may, if possible, thy pardon find
The easier towards me, or thy hatred less.
First granting, as I do, it was a weakness
In me, but incident to all our sex,
Curiosity, inquisitive, importune
Of secrets, then with like infirmity
To publish them, both common female faults ;
Was it not weakness also to make known,
For importunity, that is for nought,
Wherein consisted all thy strength and safety ?
To what I did thou show'dst me first the way.
But I to enemies revealed, and should not ;
Nor shouldst thou have trusted that to woman's frailty.
Ere I to thee, thou to thyself wast cruel.
Let weakness, then, with weakness come to parle,
So near related, or the same of kind,
Thine forgive mine ; that men may censure thine

The gentler, if severely thou exact not
More strength from me than in thyself was found.
And what if love, which thou interpret'st hate,
The jealousy of love, powerful of sway
In human hearts, nor less in mine towards thee,
Caused what I did ?   I saw thee mutable
Of fancy ; feared lest one day thou wouldst leave me
As her at Timna ; sought by all means, therefore,
How to endear, and hold thee to me firmest ;
No better way I saw than by importuning
To learn thy secrets, get into my power
The key of strength and safety.   Thou wilt say,
"Why, then, revealed ? "   I was assured by those
Who tempted me, that nothing was designed
Against thee but safe custody, and hold.
That made for me ; I knew that liberty
Would draw thee forth to perilous enterprises,
While I at home sat full of cares and fears,
Wailing thy absence in my widowed bed ;
Here I should still enjoy thee, day and night,
Mine and love's prisoner, not the Philistines',
Whole to myself, unhazarded abroad,
Fearless at home of partners in my love.
These reasons in love's law have passed for good,
Though fond and reasonless to some, perhaps ;
And love hath oft, well meaning, wrought much woe,
Yet always pity or pardon hath obtained.
Be not unlike all others, not austere
As thou art strong, inflexible as steel.
If thou in strength all mortals dost exceed,
In uncompassionate anger do not so.
   Sams. How cunningly the sorceress displays
Her own transgressions, to upbraid me mine !
That malice, not repentance, brought thee hither,
By this appears ; I gave, thou say'st, the example,
I led the way,—bitter reproach, but true ;
I to myself was false, ere thou to me.

SAMSON AGONISTES

Such pardon, therefore, as I give my folly,
Take to thy wicked deed ; which when thou seest
Impartial, self-severe, inexorable,
Thou wilt renounce thy seeking, and much rather
Confess it feigned.   Weakness is thy excuse,
And I believe it,—weakness to resist
Philistian gold.   If weakness may excuse,
What murtherer, what traitor, parricide,
Incestuous, sacrilegious, but may plead it ?
All wickedness is weakness ; that plea, therefore,
With God or man, will gain thee no remission.
But love constrained thee ! call it furious rage
To satisfy thy lust ; love seeks to have love ;
My love how couldst thou hope, who took'st the way
To raise in me inexpiable hate,
Knowing, as needs I must, by thee betrayed ?
In vain thou strivest to cover shame with shame,
Or by evasions thy crime uncover'st more.
     Dal. Since thou determinest weakness for no plea
In man or woman, though to thy own condemning,
Hear what assaults I had, what snares besides,
What sieges girt me round, ere I consented ;
Which might have awed the best resolved of men,
The constantest, to have yielded without blame.
It was not gold, as to my charge thou layest,
That wrought with me.   Thou know'st the magistrates
And princes of my country came in person,
Solicited, commanded, threatened, urged,
Adjured, by all the bonds of civil duty
And of religion, pressed how just it was,
How honourable, how glorious, to entrap
A common enemy, who had destroyed
Such numbers of our nation ; and the priest
Was not behind, but ever at my ear,
Preaching how meritorious with the gods
It would be to ensnare an irreligious
Dishonourer of Dagon.   What had I

SAMSON AGONISTES

To oppose against such powerful arguments?
Only my love of thee held long debate,
And combated in silence all these reasons
With hard contest.   At length, that grounded maxim,
So rife and celebrated in the mouths
Of wisest men, that to the public good
Private respects must yield, with grave authority
Took full possession of me, and prevailed;
Virtue, as I thought, truth, duty, so enjoining.
   Sams. I thought where all thy circling wiles would end,
In feigned religion, smooth hypocrisy!
But, had thy love, still odiously pretended,
Been, as it ought, sincere, it would have taught thee
Far other reasonings, brought forth other deeds.
I, before all the daughters of my tribe
And of my nation, chose thee from among
My enemies, loved thee, as too well thou knew'st,
Too well, unbosomed all my secrets to thee,
Not out of levity, but overpowered
By thy request, who could deny thee nothing;
Yet now am judged an enemy.   Why, then,
Didst thou at first receive me for thy husband,
Then, as since then, thy country's foe professed?
Being once a wife, for me thou wast to leave
Parents and country; nor was I their subject,
Nor under their protection, but my own;
Thou mine, not theirs.   If aught against my life
Thy country sought of thee, it sought unjustly,
Against the law of nature, law of nations;
No more thy country, but an impious crew
Of men conspiring to uphold their state
By worse, than hostile deeds, violating the ends
For which our country is a name so dear;
Not therefore to be obeyed.   But zeal moved thee;
To please thy gods thou didst it; gods unable
To acquit themselves and prosecute their foes
But by ungodly deeds, the contradiction

SAMSON AGONISTES

Of their own deity, gods cannot be;
Less therefore to be pleased, obeyed, or feared.
These false pretexts and varnished colours failing,
Bare in thy guilt, how foul must thou appear!
   Dal. In argument with men a woman ever
Goes by the worse, whatever be her cause.
   Sams. For want of words no doubt, or lack of breath!
Witness when I was worried with thy peals.
   Dal. I was a fool, too rash, and quite mistaken
In what I thought would have succeeded best.
Let me obtain forgiveness of thee, Samson;
Afford me place to show what recompense
Towards thee I intend for what I have misdone,
Misguided; only what remains past cure
Bear not too sensibly, nor still insist
To afflict thyself in vain. Though sight be lost,
Life yet hath many solaces, enjoyed
Where other senses want not their delights,
At home, in leisure and domestic ease,
Exempt from many a care and chance to which
Eyesight exposes, daily, men abroad.
I to the lords will intercede, not doubting
Their favourable ear, that I may fetch thee
From forth this loathsome prison-house, to abide
With me, where my redoubled love and care,
With nursing diligence, to me glad office,
May ever tend about thee to old age,
With all things grateful cheered, and so supplied,
That what by me thou hast lost thou least shalt miss.
   Sams. No, no; of my condition take no care;
It fits not; thou and I long since are twain.
Nor think me so unwary or accursed
To bring my feet again into the snare
Where once I have been caught. I know thy trains,
Though dearly to my cost, thy gins, and toils.
Thy fair enchanted cup, and warbling charms,
No more on me have power; their force is nulled;

SAMSON AGONISTES

So much of adder's wisdom I have learned,
To fence my ear against thy sorceries.
If in my flower of youth and strength, when all men
Loved, honoured, feared me, thou alone could hate me,
Thy husband, slight me, sell me, and forgo me,
How wouldst thou use me now, blind, and thereby
Deceivable, in most things as a child
Helpless, thence easily contemned and scorned,
And last neglected! How wouldst thou insult,
When I must live uxorious to thy will
In perfect thraldom! how again betray me,
Bearing my words and doings to the lords
To gloss upon, and censuring, frown or smile!
This jail I count the house of liberty
To thine, whose doors my feet shall never enter.

  Dal. Let me approach at least, and touch thy hand.
  Sams. Not for thy life, lest fierce remembrance wake
My sudden rage to tear thee joint by joint.
At distance I forgive thee; go with that;
Bewail thy falsehood, and the pious works
It hath brought forth to make thee memorable
Among illustrious women, faithful wives!
Cherish thy hastened widowhood with the gold
Of matrimonial treason; so farewell.

  Dal. I see thou art implacable, more deaf
To prayers, than winds and seas; yet winds to seas
Are reconciled at length, and sea to shore;
Thy anger, unappeasable, still rages,
Eternal tempests, never to be calmed.
Why do I humble thus myself, and, suing
For peace, reap nothing but repulse and hate,
Bid go with evil omen, and the brand
Of infamy upon my name denounced?
To mix with thy concernments I desist
Henceforth, nor too much disapprove my own.
Fame, if not double-faced, is double-mouthed,
And with contrary blast proclaims most deeds;

M

SAMSON AGONISTES

On both his wings, one black, the other white,
Bears greatest names in his wild aëry flight.
My name, perhaps, among the circumcised
In Dan, in Judah, and the bordering tribes,
To all posterity may stand defamed,
With malediction mentioned, and the blot
Of falsehood most unconjugal traduced.
But in my country, where I most desire,
In Ecron, Gaza, Ashdod, and in Gath,
I shall be named among the famousest
Of women, sung at solemn festivals,
Living and dead recorded, who, to save
Her country from a fierce destroyer, chose
Above the faith of wedlock bands ; my tomb
With odours visited and annual flowers ;
Not less renowned than in Mount Ephraim
Jael, who, with inhospitable guile,
Smote Sisera sleeping, through the temples nailed.
Nor shall I count it heinous to enjoy
The public marks of honour and reward,
Conferred upon me for the piety
Which to my country I was judged to have shown.
At this whoever envies or repines,
I leave him to his lot, and like my own.   [*Exit.*

   Cho. She's gone ; a manifest serpent, by her sting
Discovered in the end, till now concealed.
   Sams. So let her go ; God sent her to debase me,
And aggravate my folly, who committed
To such a viper his most sacred trust
Of secrecy, my safety, and my life.
   Cho. Yet beauty, though injurious, hath strange power,
After offence returning, to regain
Love once possessed, nor can be easily
Repulsed, without much inward passion felt,
And secret sting of amorous remorse.
   Sams. Love-quarrels oft in pleasing concord end,
Not wedlock-treachery endangering life.

SAMSON AGONISTES

Cho. It is not virtue, wisdom, valour, wit,
Strength, comeliness of shape, or amplest merit,
That woman's love can win, or long inherit ;
But what it is, hard is to say,
Harder to hit,
Which way soever men refer it,
Much like thy riddle, Samson, in one day
Or seven though one should musing sit.
   If any of these, or all, the Timnian bride
Had not so soon preferred
Thy paranymph, worthless to thee compared,
Successor in thy bed,
Nor both so loosely disallied
Their nuptials, nor this last so treacherously
Had shorn the fatal harvest of thy head.
Is it for that such outward ornament
Was lavished on their sex, that inward gifts
Were left for haste unfinished, judgment scant,
Capacity not raised to apprehend
Or value what is best
In choice, but oftest to affect the wrong ?
Or was too much of self-love mixed,
Of constancy no root infixed,
That either they love nothing, or not long ?
   Whate'er it be, to wisest men and best
Seeming at first all heavenly under virgin veil,
Soft, modest, meek, demure,
Once joined, the contrary she proves, a thorn
Intestine, far within defensive arms
A cleaving mischief, in his way to virtue
Adverse and turbulent ; or by her charms
Draws him awry enslaved
With dotage, and his sense depraved
To folly and shameful deeds, which ruin ends.
What pilot so expert but needs must wreck,
Embarked with such a steers-mate at the helm ?
   Favoured of Heaven, who finds

One virtuous, rarely found,
That in domestic good combines.
Happy that house! his way to peace is smooth.
But virtue, which breaks through all opposition,
And all temptation can remove,
Most shines and most is acceptable above.
    Therefore God's universal law
Gave to the man despotic power
Over his female in due awe,
Nor from that right to part an hour,
Smile she or lour.
So shall he least confusion draw
On his whole life, not swayed
By female usurpation, or dismayed.
    But had we best retire?   I see a storm.
    Sams. Fair days have oft contracted wind and rain.
    Cho. But this another kind of tempest brings.
    Sams. Be less abstruse; my riddling days are past.
    Cho. Look now for no enchanting voice, nor fear
The bait of honeyed words; a rougher tongue
Draws hitherward; I know him by his stride,
The giant Harapha of Gath, his look
Haughty, as is his pile high-built and proud,
Comes he in peace? What wind hath blown him hither
I less conjecture than when first I saw
The sumptuous Dalila floating this way;
His habit carries peace, his brow defiance.
    Sams. Or peace, or not, alike to me he comes.
    Cho. His fraught we soon shall know; he now arrives.
    Harapha. I come not, Samson, to condole thy chance,
As these perhaps, yet wish it had not been,
Though for no friendly intent.   I am of Gath;
Men call me Harapha, of stock renowned
As Og, or Anak, and the Emims old
That Kiriathaim held; thou know'st me now
If thou at all art known.   Much I have heard
Of thy prodigious might and feats performed,

HARAPHA

SAMSON AGONISTES

Incredible to me, in this displeased,
That I was never present on the place
Of these encounters, where we might have tried
Each other's force in camp or listed field ;
And now am come to see of whom such noise
Hath walked about, and each limb to survey,
If thy appearance answer loud report.
    Sams. The way to know were not to see, but taste.
    Har. Dost thou already single me ? I thought
Gyves and the mill had tamed thee.   Oh that fortune
Had brought me to the field where thou art famed
To have wrought such wonders with an ass's jaw !
I should have forced thee soon with other arms,
Or left thy carcass where the ass lay thrown ;
So had the glory of prowess been recovered
To Palestine, won by a Philistine
From the unforeskinned race, of whom thou bear'st
The highest name for valiant acts ; that honour,
Certain to have won by mortal duel from thee,
I lose, prevented by thy eyes put out.
    Sams. Boast not of what thou wouldst have done, but do
What then thou wouldst ; thou seest it in thy hand.
    Har. To combat with a blind man I disdain,
And thou hast need much washing to be touched.
    Sams. Such usage as your honourable lords
Afford me, assassinated and betrayed,
Who durst not with their whole united powers
In fight withstand me, single and unarmed,
Nor in the house, with chamber-ambushes
Close-banded, durst attack me, no, not sleeping,
Till they had hired a woman with their gold,
Breaking her marriage-faith, to circumvent me.
Therefore, without feigned shifts, let be assigned
Some narrow place enclosed, where sight may give thee,
Or rather flight, no great advantage on me ;
Then put on all thy gorgeous arms, thy helmet
And brigandine of brass, thy broad habergeon,

SAMSON AGONISTES

Vant-brace and greaves, and gauntlet, add thy spear,
A weaver's beam, and seven-times-folded shield;
I only with an oaken staff will meet thee,
And raise such outcries on thy clattered iron,
Which long shall not withhold me from thy head,
That in a little time, while breath remains thee,
Thou oft shall wish thyself at Gath, to boast
Again in safety what thou wouldst have done
To Samson, but shalt never see Gath more.

   Har. Thou durst not thus disparage glorious arms,
Which greatest heroes have in battle worn,
Their ornament and safety, had not spells
And black enchantments, some magician's art,
Armed thee or charmed thee strong, which thou from Heaven
Feign'dst at thy birth was given thee in thy hair,
Where strength can least abide, though all thy hairs
Were bristles ranged like those that ridge the back
Of chafed wild boars or ruffled porcupines.

   Sams. I know no spells, use no forbidden arts;
My trust is in the living God, who gave me,
At my nativity, this strength, diffused
No less through all my sinews, joints, and bones,
Than thine, while I preserved these locks unshorn,
The pledge of my unviolated vow.
For proof hereof, if Dagon be thy god,
Go to his temple, invocate his aid
With solemnest devotion, spread before him
How highly it concerns his glory now
To frustrate and dissolve these magic spells,
Which I to be the power of Israel's God
Avow, and challenge Dagon to the test,
Offering to combat thee, his champion bold,
With the utmost of his godhead seconded;
Then thou shalt see, or rather to thy sorrow
Soon feel, whose God is strongest, thine or mine.

   Har. Presume not on thy God, whate'er He be;
Thee He regards not, owns not, hath cut off

SAMSON AGONISTES

Quite from His people, and delivered up
Into thy enemies' hand, permitted them
To put out both thine eyes, and fettered send thee
Into the common prison, there to grind
Among the slaves and asses, thy comrades,
As good for nothing else, no better service
With those thy boisterous locks, no worthy match
For valour to assail, nor by the sword
Of noble warrior, so to stain his honour,
But by the barber's razor best subdued.

Sams. All these indignities, for such they are
From thine, these evils I deserve and more,
Acknowledge them from God inflicted on me
Justly, yet despair not of His final pardon,
Whose ear is ever open, and His eye
Gracious to re-admit the suppliant;
In confidence whereof I once again
Defy thee to the trial of mortal fight,
By combat to decide whose god is God,
Thine, or whom I with Israel's sons adore.

Har. Fair honour that thou dost thy God, in trusting
He will accept thee to defend His cause,
A murtherer, a revolter, and a robber!

Sams. Tongue-doughty giant, how dost thou prove
me these?

Har. Is not thy nation subject to our lords?
Their magistrates confessed it when they took thee
As a league-breaker, and delivered bound
Into our hands; for hadst thou not committed
Notorious murder on those thirty men
At Ascalon, who never did thee harm,
Then, like a robber, stripp'dst them of their robes?
The Philistines, when thou hadst broke the league,
Went up with armed powers, thee only seeking,
To others did no violence nor spoil.

Sams. Among the daughters of the Philistines
I chose a wife, which argued me no foe,

169

SAMSON AGONISTES

And in your city held my nuptial feast;
But your ill-meaning politician lords,
Under pretence of bridal friends and guests,
Appointed to await me thirty spies,
Who, threatening cruel death, constrained the bride
To wring from me and tell to them my secret,
That solved the riddle which I had proposed.
When I perceived all set on enmity,
As on my enemies, wherever chanced,
I used hostility, and took their spoil,
To pay my underminers in their coin.
My nation was subjected to your lords!
It was the force of conquest; force with force
Is well ejected when the conquered can.
But I, a private person, whom my country
As a league-breaker gave up bound, presumed
Single rebellion, and did hostile acts.
I was no private, but a person raised
With strength sufficient, and command from Heaven,
To free my country; if their servile minds
Me, their deliverer sent, would not receive,
But to their masters gave me up for nought,
The unworthier they; whence to this day they serve.
I was to do my part from Heaven assigned,
And had performed it, if my known offence
Had not disabled me, not all your force.
These shifts refuted, answer thy appellant,
Though by his blindness maimed for high attempts,
Who now defies thee thrice to single fight,
As a petty enterprise of small enforce.
  Har. With thee, a man condemned, a slave enrolled,
Due by the law to capital punishment?
To fight with thee no man of arms will deign.
  Sams. Camest thou for this, vain boaster, to survey me,
To descant on my strength, and give thy verdict?
Come nearer; part not hence so slight informed;
But take good heed my hand survey not thee.

Har. O Baal-zebub! can my ears unused
Hear these dishonours, and not render death?
  Sams. No man withholds thee; nothing from thy hand
Fear I incurable; bring up thy van,
My heels are fettered, but my fist is free.
  Har. This insolence other kind of answer fits.
  Sams. Go, baffled coward, lest I run upon thee,
Though in these chains, bulk without spirit vast,
And with one buffet lay thy structure low,
Or swing thee in the air, then dash thee down,
To the hazard of thy brains and shattered sides.
  Har. By Astaroth, ere long thou shalt lament
These braveries in irons loaden on thee.   [*Exit.*
  Cho. His giantship is gone somewhat crestfallen,
Stalking with less unconscionable strides,
And lower looks, but in a sultry chafe.
  Sams. I dread him not, nor all his giant brood,
Though fame divulge him father of five sons,
All of gigantic size, Goliah chief.
  Cho. He will directly to the lords, I fear,
And with malicious counsel stir them up
Some way or other yet further to afflict thee.
  Sams. He must allege some cause, and offered fight
Will not dare mention, lest a question rise
Whether he durst accept the offer or not;
And, that he durst not, plain enough appeared.
Much more affliction than already felt
They cannot well impose, nor I sustain,
If they intend advantage of my labours,
The work of many hands, which earns my keeping
With no small profit daily to my owners.
But come what will, my deadliest foe will prove
My speediest friend, by death to rid me hence;
The worst that he can give, to me the best.
Yet so it may fall out, because their end
Is hate, not help to me, it may with mine
Draw their own ruin who attempt the deed.

SAMSON AGONISTES

Cho. Oh, how comely it is, and how reviving
To the spirits of just men long oppressed,
When God into the hands of their deliverer
Puts invincible might
To quell the mighty of the earth, the oppressor,
The brute and boisterous force of violent men,
Hardy and industrious to support
Tyrannic power, but raging to pursue
The righteous, and all such as honour truth ;
He all their ammunition
And feats of war defeats,
With plain heroic magnitude of mind
And celestial vigour armed ;
Their armouries and magazines contemns,
Renders them useless, while,
With winged expedition,
Swift as the lightning glance He executes
His errand on the wicked, who, surprised,
Lose their defence, distracted and amazed.
    But patience is more oft the exercise
Of saints, the trial of their fortitude,
Making them each his own deliverer,
And victor over all
That tyranny or fortune can inflict.
Either of these is in thy lot,
Samson, with might endued
Above the sons of men ; but sight bereaved
May chance to number thee with those
Whom patience finally must crown.
    This idol's day hath been to thee no day of rest,
Labouring thy mind
More than the working day thy hands.
And yet, perhaps, more trouble is behind,
For I descry this way
Some other tending ; in his hand
A sceptre or quaint staff he bears,
Comes on amain, speed in his look.

SAMSON AGONISTES

By his habit I discern him now
A public officer, and now at hand.
His message will be short and voluble.
  Officer. Hebrews, the prisoner Samson here I seek.
  Cho. His manacles remark him, there he sits.
  Off. Samson, to thee our lords thus bid me say:
This day to Dagon is a solemn feast,
With sacrifices, triumph, pomp, and games ;
Thy strength they know surpassing human rate,
And now some public proof thereof require
To honour this great feast, and great assembly.
Rise, therefore, with all speed, and come along,
Where I will see thee heartened and fresh clad,
To appear as fits before the illustrious lords.
  Sams. Thou knowest I am a Hebrew, therefore tell them
Our law forbids at their religious rites
My presence ; for that cause I cannot come.
  Off. This answer, be assured, will not content them.
  Sams. Have they not sword-players, and every sort
Of gymnic artists, wrestlers, riders, runners,
Jugglers, and dancers, antics, mummers, mimics,
But they must pick me out, with shackles tired,
And over-laboured at their public mill,
To make them sport with blind activity?
Do they not seek occasion of new quarrels,
On my refusal, to distress me more,
Or make a game of my calamities?
Return the way thou camest ; I will not come.
  Off. Regard thyself; this will offend them highly.
  Sams. Myself? my conscience, and internal peace.
Can they think me so broken, so debased
With corporal servitude, that my mind ever
Will condescend to such absurd commands,——
Although their drudge, to be their fool or jester,
And in my midst of sorrow and heart-grief
To show them feats, and play before their god,
The worst of all indignities, yet on me

173

Joined with extreme contempt? I will not come.

Off. My message was imposed on me with speed,
Brooks no delay; is this thy resolution?

Sams. So take it with what speed thy message needs.

Off. I am sorry what this stoutness will produce. [*Exit.*

Sams. Perhaps thou shalt have cause to sorrow indeed.

Cho. Consider, Samson; matters now are strained
Up to the height, whether to hold or break.
He's gone, and who knows how he may report
Thy words by adding fuel to the flame?
Expect another message, more imperious,
More lordly thundering than thou well wilt bear.

Sams. Shall I abuse this consecrated gift
Of strength again returning with my hair
After my great transgression, so requite
Favour renewed, and add a greater sin
By prostituting holy things to idols,
A Nazarite, in place abominable,
Vaunting my strength in honour to their Dagon?
Besides, how vile, contemptible, ridiculous!
What act more execrably unclean, profane?

Cho. Yet with this strength thou servest the Philistines,
Idolatrous, uncircumcised, unclean.

Sams. Not in their idol-worship, but by labour,
Honest and lawful, to deserve my food
Of those who have me in their civil power.

Cho. Where the heart joins not, outward acts defile not.

Sams. Where outward force constrains, the sentence hold:
But who constrains me to the temple of Dagon,
Not dragging? The Philistian lords command;—
Commands are no constraints. If I obey them,
I do it freely, venturing to displease
God for the fear of man, and man prefer,
Set God behind; which, in His jealousy,
Shall never, unrepented, find forgiveness.
Yet that He may dispense with me, or thee,
Present in temples at idolatrous rites

SAMSON AGONISTES

For some important cause, thou need'st not doubt.
  Cho. How thou wilt here come off surmounts my reach.
  Sams. Be of good courage ; I begin to feel
Some rousing motions in me, which dispose
To something extraordinary my thoughts.
I with this messenger will go along,—
Nothing to do, be sure, that may dishonour
Our law, or stain my vow of Nazarite.
If there be aught of presage in the mind,
This day will be remarkable in my life
By some great act, or of my days the last.
  Cho. In time thou hast resolved,—the man returns.
  Off. Samson, this second message from our lords
To thee I am bid say : Art thou our slave,
Our captive, at the public mill our drudge,
And darest thou, at our sending and command,
Dispute thy coming ? Come without delay,
Or we shall find such engines to assail
And hamper thee, as thou shalt come of force,
Though thou wert firmlier fastened than a rock.
  Sams. I could be well content to try their art,
Which to no few of them would prove pernicious.
Yet, knowing their advantages too many,
Because they shall not trail me through their streets
Like a wild beast, I am content to go.
Masters' commands come with a power resistless
To such as owe them absolute subjection ;
And for a life who will not change his purpose?
(So mutable are all the ways of men !)
Yet this be sure, in nothing to comply
Scandalous or forbidden in our law.
  Off. I praise thy resolution ; doff these links ;
By this compliance thou wilt win the lords
To favour, and perhaps to set thee free.
  Sams. Brethren, farewell ; your company along
I will not wish, lest it, perhaps, offend them
To see me girt with friends ; and how the sight

Of me, as of a common enemy,
So dreaded once, may now exasperate them,
I know not; lords are lordliest in their wine;
And the well-feasted priest then soonest fired
With zeal, if aught religion seem concerned;
No less the people, on their holy-days,
Impetuous, insolent, unquenchable.
Happen what may, of me expect to hear
Nothing dishonourable, impure, unworthy
Our God, our law, my nation, or myself;
The last of me or no I cannot warrant.   [*Exit.*

   Cho. Go, and the Holy One
Of Israel be thy guide
To what may serve His glory best, and spread His name
Great among the heathen round;
Send thee the Angel of thy birth, to stand
Fast by thy side, who, from thy father's field,
Rode up in flames after his message told
Of thy conception, and be now a shield
Of fire; that Spirit, that first rushed on thee
In the camp of Dan,
Be efficacious in thee now at need!
For never was from Heaven imparted
Measure of strength so great to mortal seed,
As in thy wondrous actions hath been seen.
But wherefore comes old Manoah in such haste
With youthful steps? much livelier than erewhile
He seems; supposing here to find his son,
Or of him bringing to us some glad news.

   Man. Peace with you, brethren; my inducement hither
Was not at present here to find my son,
By order of the lords new-parted hence
To come and play before them at their feast.
I heard all as I came; the city rings,
And numbers thither flock. I had no will,
Lest I should see him forced to things unseemly.
But that which moved my coming now was chiefly

SAMSON AND THE OFFICER

To give ye part with me what hope I have
With good success to work his liberty.
  Cho. That hope would much rejoice us to partake
With thee. Say, reverend sire ; we thirst to hear.
  Man. I have attempted, one by one, the lords
Either at home, or through the high street passing,
With supplication prone and father's tears,
To accept of ransom for my son, their prisoner.
Some much averse I found and wondrous harsh,
Contemptuous, proud, set on revenge and spite,
That part most reverenced Dagon and his priests ;
Others more moderate seeming, but their aim
Private reward, for which both God and State
They easily would set to sale ; a third
More generous far and civil, who confessed
They had enough revenged, having reduced
Their foe to misery beneath their fears ;
The rest was magnanimity to remit,
If some convenient ransom were proposed.
What noise or shout was that? it tore the sky.
  Cho. Doubtless, the people shouting to behold
Their once great dread, captive and blind before them,
Or at some proof of strength before them shown.
  Man. His ransom, if my whole inheritance
May compass it, shall willingly be paid
And numbered down ; much rather I shall choose
To live the poorest in my tribe, than richest
And he in that calamitous prison left.
No, I am fixed not to part hence without him.
For his redemption all my patrimony,
If need be, I am ready to forgo
And quit ; not wanting him, I shall want nothing.
  Cho. Fathers are wont to lay up for their sons,
Thou for thy son art bent to lay out all ;
Sons wont to nurse their parents in old age,
Thou in old age carest how to nurse thy son,
Made older than thy age through eyesight lost.

SAMSON AGONISTES

Man. It shall be my delight to tend his eyes,
And view him sitting in his house, ennobled
With all those high exploits by him achieved,
And on his shoulders waving down those locks
That of a nation armed the strength contained.
And I persuade me, God had not permitted
His strength again to grow up with his hair,
Garrisoned round about him like a camp
Of faithful soldiery, were not His purpose
To use him further yet in some great service,
Not to sit idle with so great a gift
Useless, and thence ridiculous, about him.
And since his strength with eyesight was not lost,
God will restore him eyesight to his strength.
   Cho. Thy hopes are not ill founded, nor seem vain
Of his delivery, and thy joy thereon,
Conceived, agreeable to a father's love,
In both which we, as next, participate.
   Man. I know your friendly minds, and—oh, what noise!
Mercy of Heaven! what hideous noise was that!
Horribly loud, unlike the former shout.
   Cho. Noise call you it, or universal groan,
As if the whole inhabitation perished?
Blood, death, and deathful deeds, are in that noise;
Ruin, destruction at the utmost point.
   Man. Of ruin, indeed, methought I heard the noise.
Oh! it continues; they have slain my son!
   Cho. Thy son is rather slaying them; that outcry
From slaughter of one foe could not ascend.
   Man. Some dismal accident it needs must be.
What shall we do, stay here, or run and see?
   Cho. Best keep together here, lest, running thither,
We, unawares, run into danger's mouth.
This evil on the Philistines is fallen;
From whom could else a general cry be heard?
The sufferers, then, will scarce molest us here;
From other hands we need not much to fear.

MANOAH AND THE CHORUS

SAMSON AGONISTES

What if, his eyesight (for to Israel's God
Nothing is hard) by miracle restored,
He now be dealing dole among his foes,
And over heaps of slaughtered walk his way?
   Man. That were a joy presumptuous to be thought.
   Cho. Yet God hath wrought things as incredible
For His people of old ; what hinders now?
   Man. He can, I know, but doubt to think he will.
Yet hope would fain subscribe, and tempts belief.
A little stay will bring some notice hither.
   Cho. Of good or bad so great, of bad the sooner ;
For evil news rides post, while good news baits.
And to our wish I see one hither speeding,
A Hebrew, as I guess, and of our tribe.
   Messenger. Oh, whither shall I run, or which way fly
The sight of this so horrid spectacle,
Which erst my eyes beheld, and yet behold?
For dire imagination still pursues me.
But Providence or instinct of nature seems,
Or reason, though disturbed, and scarce consulted,
To have guided me aright, I know not how,
To thee first, reverend Manoah, and to these
My countrymen, whom here I knew remaining,
As at some distance from the place of horror,
So in the sad event too much concerned.
   Man. The accident was loud, and here before thee
With rueful cry, yet what it was we hear not ;
No preface needs, thou seest we long to know.
   Mess. It would burst forth, but I recover breath,
And sense distract, to know well what I utter.
   Man. Tell us the sum, the circumstance defer.
   Mess. Gaza yet stands, but all her sons are fallen,
All in a moment overwhelmed and fallen.
   Man. Sad ! but thou know'st to Israelites not saddest
The desolation of a hostile city.
   Mess. Feed on that first ; there may in grief be surfeit.
   Man. Relate by whom.

SAMSON AGONISTES

Mess.   By Samson.
Man.   That still lessens
The sorrow, and converts it nigh to joy.
  Mess. Ah! Manoah, I refrain too suddenly
To utter what will come at last too soon;
Lest evil tidings, with too rude irruption
Hitting thy aged ear, should pierce too deep.
  Man. Suspense in news is torture; speak them out.
  Mess. Take then the worst, in brief. Samson is dead.
  Man. The worst, indeed! Oh, all my hope's defeated
To free him hence! but Death, who sets all free,
Hath paid his ransom now and full discharge.
What windy joy this day had I conceived,
Hopeful of his delivery, which now proves
Abortive as the first-born bloom of spring
Nipt with the lagging rear of winter's frost!
Yet, ere I give the reins to grief, say, first,
How died he; death to life is crown or shame.
All by him fell, thou say'st; by whom fell he?
What glorious hand gave Samson his death's wound?
  Mess. Unwounded of his enemies he fell.
  Man. Wearied with slaughter, then, or how? explain.
  Mess. By his own hands.
  Man.   Self-violence? what cause
Brought him so soon at variance with himself
Among his foes?
  Mess.   Inevitable cause,—
At once both to destroy and be destroyed;
The edifice, where all were met to see him,
Upon their heads and on his own he pulled.
  Man. Oh, lastly over-strong against thyself!
A dreadful way thou took'st to thy revenge.
More than enough we know; but while things yet
Are in confusion, give us, if thou canst,
Eye-witness of what first or last was done,
Relation more particular and distinct.
  Mess. Occasions drew me early to this city;

184

SAMSON AGONISTES

And, as the gates I entered with sun-rise,
The morning trumpets festival proclaimed
Through each high street.   Little I had despatched,
When all abroad was rumoured that this day
Samson should be brought forth to show the people
Proof of his mighty strength in feats and games.
I sorrowed at his captive state, but minded
Not to be absent at that spectacle.
The building was a spacious theatre,
Half round, on two main pillars vaulted high,
With seats where all the lords, and each degree
Of sort might sit in order to behold ;
The other side was open, where the throng,
On banks and scaffolds, under sky might stand ;
I, among these, aloof obscurely stood.
The feast and noon grew high, and sacrifice
Had filled their hearts with mirth, high cheer and wine,
When to their sports they turned.   Immediately
Was Samson as a public servant brought,
In their state livery clad ; before him pipes
And timbrels ; on each side went armed guards,
Both horse and foot, before him and behind
Archers and slingers, cataphracts and spears.
At sight of him the people with a shout
Rifted the air, clamouring their god with praise,
Who had made their dreadful enemy their thrall.
He patient, but undaunted where they led him,
Came to the place ; and what was set before him,
Which without help of eye might be assayed,
To heave, pull, draw, or break, he still performed
All with incredible stupendous force,
None daring to appear antagonist.
At length, for intermission sake, they led him
Between the pillars ; he his guide requested,
(For so from such as nearer stood we heard)
As over-tired, to let him lean a while
With both his arms on those two massy pillars,

SAMSON AGONISTES

That to the arched roof gave main support.
He, unsuspicious, led him ; which, when Samson
Felt in his arms, with head awhile inclined,
And eyes fast fixed, he stood, as one who prayed,
Or some great matter in his mind revolved.
At last, with head erect, thus cried aloud :—
" Hitherto, lords, what your commands imposed
I have performed, as reason was, obeying,
Not without wonder or delight beheld ;
Now, of my own accord, such other trial
I mean to show you of my strength, yet greater,
As with amaze shall strike all who behold."
This uttered, straining all his nerves, he bowed ;
As with the force of winds and waters pent,
When mountains tremble, those two massy pillars
With horrible convulsion to and fro
He tugged, he shook, till down they came, and drew
The whole roof after them with burst of thunder
Upon the heads of all who sat beneath,
Lords, ladies, captains, counsellors, or priests,
Their choice nobility and flower, not only
Of this, but each Philistian city round,
Met from all parts to solemnize this feast.
Samson, with these immixed, inevitably
Pulled down the same destruction on himself ;
The vulgar only scaped who stood without.
   Cho. O dearly bought revenge, yet glorious !
Living or dying thou hast fulfilled
The work for which thou wast foretold
To Israel, and now liest victorious
Among thy slain, self-killed,
Not willingly, but tangled in the fold
Of dire necessity, whose law in death conjoined
Thee with thy slaughtered foes, in number more
Than all thy life had slain before.
   Semicho. While their hearts were jocund and sublime,
Drunk with idolatry, drunk with wine,

SAMSON IN THE TEMPLE

And fat regorged of bulls and goats,
Chaunting their idol, and preferring
Before our living Dread, who dwells
In Silo, his bright sanctuary,
Among them he a spirit of frenzy sent,
Who hurt their minds,
And urged them on with mad desire
To call in haste for their destroyer;
They, only set on sport and play,
Unweetingly importuned
Their own destruction to come speedy upon them.
So fond are mortal men,
Fallen into wrath divine,
As their own ruin on themselves to invite,
Insensate left, or to sense reprobate,
And with blindness internal struck.

    Semicho. But he, though blind of sight,
Despised, and thought extinguished quite,
With inward eyes illuminated,
His fiery virtue roused
From under ashes into sudden flame,
And as an evening dragon came,
Assailant on the perched roosts
And nests in order ranged
Of tame villatic fowl; but as an eagle
His cloudless thunder bolted on their heads.
So Virtue, given for lost,
Depressed and overthrown, as seemed,
Like that self-begotten bird
In the Arabian woods embost,
That no second knows nor third,
And lay erewhile a holocaust,
From out her ashy womb now teemed.
Revives, reflourishes, then vigorous most
When most unactive deemed;
And, though her body die, her fame survives,
A secular bird, ages of lives.

SAMSON AGONISTES

Man. Come, come, no time for lamentation now,
Nor much more cause.   Samson hath quit himself
Like Samson, and heroicly hath finished
A life heroic, on his enemies
Fully revenged ; hath left them years of mourning
And lamentation to the sons of Caphtor
Through all Philistian bounds ; to Israel
Honour hath left and freedom, let but them
Find courage to lay hold on this occasion ;
To himself and father's house, eternal fame ;
And, which is best and happiest yet, all this
With God not parted from him, as was feared,
But favouring and assisting to the end.
Nothing is here for tears, nothing to wail
Or knock the breast ; no weakness, no contempt,
Dispraise, or blame ; nothing but well and fair,
And what may quiet us in a death so noble.
Let us go find the body where it lies
Soaked in his enemies' blood, and from the stream
With lavers pure, and cleansing herbs, wash off
The clotted gore.   I, with what speed the while,
(Gaza is not in plight to say us nay),
Will send for all my kindred, all my friends,
To fetch him hence, and solemnly attend,
With silent obsequy, and funeral train,
Home to his father's house ; there will I build him
A monument, and plant it round with shade
Of laurel ever green, and branching palm,
With all his trophies hung, and acts enrolled
In copious legend, or sweet lyric song.
Thither shall all the valiant youth resort,
And from his memory inflame their breasts
To matchless valour, and adventures high ;
The virgins also shall, on feastful days,
Visit his tomb with flowers, only bewailing
His lot unfortunate in nuptial choice,
From whence captivity and loss of eyes.

SAMSON MOURNED

SAMSON AGONISTES

Cho. All is best, though we oft doubt
What the unsearchable dispose
Of Highest Wisdom brings about,
And ever best found in the close.
Oft He seems to hide His face,
But unexpectedly returns,
And to His faithful champion hath in place
Bore witness gloriously ; whence Gaza mourns,
And all that band them to resist
His uncontrollable intent.
His servants He, with new acquist
Of true experience from this great event,
With peace and consolation hath dismissed,
And calm of mind, all passion spent.

SONNETS

To the Nightin- gale.

O NIGHTINGALE, that on yon bloomy spray,
   Warblest at eve, when all the woods are still,
   Thou with fresh hope the lover's heart dost fill,
While the jolly Hours lead on propitious May;
Thy liquid notes that close the eye of day,
   First heard before the shallow cuckoo's bill,
   Portend success in love. Oh, if Jove's will
Have linked that amorous power to thy soft lay
Now timely sing, ere the rude bird of hate
   Foretell my hopeless doom, in some grove nigh;
As thou from year to year hast sung too late
   For my relief, yet hadst no reason why:
Whether the Muse, or Love, call thee his mate,
   Both them I serve, and of their train am I.

SONNETS

ON HIS BEING ARRIVED AT THE AGE
OF TWENTY-THREE

How soon hath Time, the subtle thief of youth,
  Stolen on his wing my three-and-twentieth year!
  My hasting days fly on with full career,
But my late spring no bud or blossom shew'th.
Perhaps my semblance might deceive the truth
  That I to manhood am arrived so near;
  And inward ripeness doth much less appear,
That some more timely-happy spirits endu'th.
  Yet, be it less or more, or soon or slow,
It shall be still in strictest measure even
  To that same lot, however mean or high,
Toward which Time leads me, and the will of Heaven;
  All is, if I have grace to use it so,
  As ever in my great Task-Master's eye.

WHEN THE ASSAULT WAS INTENDED
TO THE CITY

Captain, or Colonel, or Knight-in-arms,
  Whose chance on these defenceless doors may seize,
  If deed of honour did thee ever please,
Guard them, and him within protect from harms.
He can requite thee, for he knows the charms
  That call fame on such gentle acts as these,
  And he can spread thy name o'er lands and seas,
Whatever clime the sun's bright circle warms.
  Lift not thy spear against the Muse's bower;
The great Emathian conqueror bid spare
  The house of Pindarus, when temple and tower
Went to the ground; and the repeated air
  Of sad Electra's poet had the power
To save the Athenian walls from ruin bare.

SONNETS

TO A VIRTUOUS YOUNG LADY

LADY, that in the prime of earliest Youth
  Wisely hast shunned the broad way and the green,
  And with those few art eminently seen,
That labour up the hill of heavenly Truth,
The better part with Mary and with Ruth
  Chosen thou hast ; and they that overween,
  And at thy growing virtues fret their spleen,
No anger find in thee, but pity and ruth.
  Thy care is fixed, and zealously attends
To fill thy odorous lamp, with deeds of light,
  And hope that reaps not shame. Therefore be sure
  Thou, when the Bridegroom with his feastful friends
Passes to bliss at the mid-hour of night,
  Hast gained thy entrance, Virgin wise and pure.

TO THE LADY MARGARET LEY

DAUGHTER to that good Earl, once President
  Of England's Council and her Treasury,
  Who lived in both unstained with gold or fee,
And left them both, more in himself content,
Till the sad breaking of that Parliament
  Broke him, as that dishonest victory
  At Chæronea, fatal to liberty,
Killed with report that old man eloquent.
  Though later born than to have known the days
Wherein your father flourished, yet by you,
  Madam, methinks, I see him living yet ;
  So well your words his noble virtues praise,
That all both judge you to relate them true
  And to possess them, honoured Margaret.

SONNETS

ON THE DETRACTION WHICH FOLLOWED UPON MY WRITING CERTAIN TREATISES

A BOOK was writ of late called *Tetrachordon,*
    And woven close, both matter, form and style ;
    The subject new ; it walked the town a while,
Numbering good intellects, now seldom pored on.
Cries the stall reader, " Bless us ! what a word on
    A title-page is this ! " and some in file
    Stand spelling false, while one might walk to Mile-
End Green.   Why, is it harder, sirs, than Gordon,
    Colkitto, or Macdonald, or Galasp ?
Those rugged names to our like mouths grow sleek,
    That would have made Quintilian stare and gasp.
Thy age, like ours, O soul of Sir John Cheek,
    Hated not learning worse than toad or asp,
When thou taught'st Cambridge and King Edward Greek.

ON THE SAME

I DID but prompt the age to quit their clogs
    By the known rules of ancient liberty,
    When straight a barbarous noise environs me
Of owls and cuckoos, asses, apes, and dogs ;
As when those hinds that were transformed to frogs
    Railed at Latona's twin-born progeny,
    Which after held the sun and moon in fee.
But this is got by casting pearl to hogs,
That bawl for freedom in their senseless mood,
    And still revolt when Truth would set them free.
    Licence they mean when they cry *Liberty ;*
For who loves that must first be wise and good ;
    But from that mark how far they rove we see,
For all this waste of wealth and loss of blood.

SONNETS

TO MR. H. LAWES ON HIS AIRS

HARRY, whose tuneful and well-measured song
  First taught our English music how to span
  Words with just note and accent, not to scan
With Midas' ears, committing short and long,
Thy worth and skill exempts thee from the throng,
  With praise enough for envy to look wan ;
  To after-age thou shalt be writ the man
That with smooth air couldst humour best our tongue.
Thou honourest verse, and verse must lend her wing
  To honour thee, the priest of Phœbus' quire,
    That tunest their happiest lines in hymn or story.
  Dante shall give Fame leave to set thee higher
Than his Casella, whom he wooed to sing,
    Met in the milder shades of Purgatory.

ON THE RELIGIOUS MEMORY OF MRS. CATHERINE THOMPSON, MY CHRISTIAN FRIEND,

DECEASED 16 DEC., 1646

WHEN Faith and Love, which parted from thee never,
  Had ripened thy just soul to dwell with God,
  Meekly thou didst resign this earthy load
Of death called life, which us from life doth sever.
Thy works, and alms, and all thy good endeavour,
  Stayed not behind nor in the grave were trod ;
  But, as Faith pointed upward with her golden rod,
Followed thee up to joy and bliss for ever.
  Love led them on, and Faith, who knew them best
Thy handmaids, clad them o'er with purple beams,
  And azure wings, that up they flew so drest,
And spake the truth of thee on glorious themes
  Before the Judge, who thenceforth bid thee rest,
And drink thy fill of pure immortal streams.

SONNETS

TO THE LORD GENERAL FAIRFAX

FAIRFAX, whose name in arms through Europe rings,
  Filling each mouth with envy or with praise,
  And all her jealous monarchs with amaze,
And rumours loud that daunt remotest kings,
Thy firm unshaken virtue ever brings
  Victory home, though new rebellions raise
  Their hydra heads, and the false North displays
Her broken league to imp their serpent wings.
  O yet a nobler task awaits thy hand
(For what can war but endless war still breed?)
Till truth and right from violence be freed,
  And public faith cleared from the shameful brand
Of public fraud. In vain doth Valour bleed,
  While Avarice and Rapine share the land.

TO THE LORD GENERAL CROMWELL,
MAY, 1652

*On the Proposals of certain Ministers of the Committee
for the Propagation of the Gospel*

CROMWELL, our chief of men, who through a cloud
  Not of war only, but detractions rude,
  Guided by faith and matchless fortitude,
To peace and truth thy glorious way hast ploughed,
And on the neck of crowned Fortune proud
  Hast reared God's trophies, and his work pursued,
  While Darwen stream, with blood of Scots imbrued,
And Dunbar field resounds thy praises loud,
And Worcester's laureate wreath. Yet much remains
  To conquer still; Peace hath her victories
  No less renowned than War; new foes arise,
Threatening to bind our souls with secular chains.
  Help us to save free conscience from the paw
  Of hireling wolves, whose Gospel is their maw.

SONNETS

TO SIR HENRY VANE THE YOUNGER

VANE, young in years, but in sage counsel old,
  Than whom a better senator ne'er held
  The helm of Rome, when gowns, not arms, repelled
The fierce Epirot and the African bold,
Whether to settle peace, or to unfold
  The drift of hollow states hard to be spelled ;
  Then to advise how war may best upheld
Move by her two main nerves, iron and gold,
In all her equipage ; besides, to know
  Both spiritual power and civil, what each means,
    What severs each, thou hast learned, which few
      have done.
The bounds of either sword to thee we owe ;
  Therefore on thy firm hand Religion leans
    In peace, and reckons thee her eldest son.

ON THE LATE MASSACRE IN PIEDMONT

AVENGE, O Lord, thy slaughtered saints, whose bones
  Lie scattered on the Alpine mountains cold ;
  Even them who kept thy truth so pure of old,
When all our fathers worshipped stocks and stones,
Forget not ; in thy book record their groans
  Who were thy sheep, and in their ancient fold
  Slain by the bloody Piedmontese, that rolled
Mother with infant down the rocks.   Their moans
  The vales redoubled to the hills, and they
To heaven.   Their martyred blood and ashes sow
  O'er all the Italian fields, where still doth sway
The triple tyrant ; that from these may grow
  A hundredfold, who, having learnt thy way,
Early may fly the Babylonian woe.

On his Blindness.

WHEN I consider how my light is spent
  Ere half my days in this dark world and wide,
  And that one talent which is death to hide
Lodged with me useless, though my soul more bent
To serve therewith my Maker, and present
  My true account, lest He, returning, chide;
  "Doth God exact day-labour, light denied?"
I fondly ask. But Patience, to prevent
That murmur, soon replies: "God doth not need
  Either men's work, or his own gifts. Who best
    Bear his mild yoke, they serve him best. His state
Is kingly; thousands at his bidding speed,
  And post o'er land and ocean without rest;
    They also serve who only stand and wait."

SONNETS

TO MR. LAWRENCE

LAWRENCE, of virtuous father virtuous son,
    Now that the fields are dank, and ways are mire,
    Where shall we sometimes meet, and by the fire
    Help waste a sullen day, what may be won
From the hard season gaining?   Time will run
    On smoother, till Favonius re-inspire
    The frozen earth, and clothe in fresh attire
    The lily and rose, that neither sowed nor spun.
What neat repast shall feast us, light and choice,
    Of Attic taste, with wine, whence we may rise
    To hear the lute well touched, or artful voice
Warble immortal notes and Tuscan air?
    He who of those delights can judge, and spare
    To interpose them oft, is not unwise.

TO CYRIACK SKINNER

CYRIACK, whose grandsire on the royal bench
    Of British Themis, with no mean applause,
    Pronounced, and in his volumes taught, our laws,
    Which others at their bar so often wrench,
To-day deep thoughts resolve with me to drench
    In mirth that after no repenting draws ;
    Let Euclid rest, and Archimedes pause,
    And what the Swede intend, and what the French.
To measure life learn thou betimes, and know
    Toward solid good what leads the nearest way ;
    For other things mild Heaven a time ordains,
And disapproves that care, though wise in show,
    That with superfluous burden loads the day,
    And, when God sends a cheerful hour, refrains.

SONNETS

TO THE SAME

CYRIACK, this three years' day these eyes, though clear,
  To outward view, of blemish or of spot,
  Bereft of light, their seeing have forgot ;
  Nor to their idle orbs doth sight appear
Of sun, or moon, or star, throughout the year,
  Or man, or woman. Yet I argue not
  Against Heaven's hand or will, nor bate a jot
  Of heart or hope, but still bear up and steer
Right onward. What supports me, dost thou ask ?
  The conscience, friend, to have lost them overplied
  In Liberty's defence, my noble task,
Of which all Europe rings from side to side.
  This thought might lead me through the world's
     vain mask
  Content, though blind, had I no better guide.

ON HIS DECEASED WIFE

METHOUGHT I saw my late espousèd saint
  Brought to me like Alcestis from the grave,
  Whom Jove's great son to her glad husband gave,
  Rescued from death by force, though pale and faint.
Mine, as whom washed from spot of child-bed taint
  Purification in the old law did save,
  And such, as yet once more I trust to have
  Full sight of her in Heaven without restraint,
Came vested all in white, pure as her mind.
  Her face was veiled ; yet to my fancied sight
  Love, sweetness, goodness, in her person shined
So clear as in no face with more delight.
  But, oh ! as to embrace me she inclined,
  I waked, she fled, and day brought back my night.

CHISWICK PRESS:—CHARLES WHITTINGHAM AND CO.
TOOKS COURT, CHANCERY LANE, LONDON.

Lightning Source UK Ltd.
Milton Keynes UK
UKOW03f1436240914

239096UK00001B/33/A